PSYCHOPATHS

Carolyn Gemini

5/12/2020

PSYCHOPATHS

Yesterday, Today, and Tomorrow

TEXE MARRS

RCP RiverCrest Publishing
4819 R.O. Drive, Suite 102, Spicewood, TX 78669

ACKNOWLEDGEMENTS

To my wife and confidant, Wanda Marrs, goes all my love and gratefulness.

Many of the people whom the author describes in this book as psychopaths have not been clinically diagnosed as psychopaths. Their inclusion in this book by the author is based on his personal evaluation and opinion.

Psychopaths: Yesterday, Today, and Tomorrow

Second Printing, 2020

Copyright © 2020 by RiverCrest Publishing. Published by RiverCrest Publishing, 4819 R. O. Drive, Suite 102, Spicewood, Texas 78669.

All Scripture quotations are from the King James Version of the Holy Bible

Cover design: Sandra Myers

Printed in the United States of America

Library of Congress Catalog Card Number 2019951280

Categories: 1. Psychology   2. Sociology
               3. Politics

ISBN-13: 978-1-930004-18-4

The old world is dying, and the new
world struggles to be born; now is
the time of monsters

— *Antonio Gramsci* —

OTHER BOOKS BY TEXE MARRS

Voices From the Dead: The Dark Rituals and Hidden Worship of the Masonic Lodge

Hell's Mirror: Global Empire of the Illuminati Builders

Feast of the Beast

The Destroyer: The Antichrist Is At Hand

Churches and Pastors Gone Wild!: America's Christian Establishment Has Gone Berserk!

DNA Science and the Jewish Bloodline

Robot Alchemy: Androids, Cyborgs, and the Magic of Artificial Life

Conspiracy of the Six-Pointed Star: Eye-opening Revelations and Forbidden Knowledge About Israel, the Jews, Zionism, and the Rothschilds

Conspiracy World: A Truthteller's Compendium of Eye-Opening Revelations and Forbidden Knowledge

Mysterious Monuments: Encyclopedia of Secret Illuminati Designs, Masonic Architecture, and Occult Places

Codex Magica: Secret Signs, Mysterious Symbols and Hidden Codes of the Illuminati

Days of Hunger, Days of Chaos

Project L.U.C.I.D.: The Beast 666 Universal Human Control System

Circle of Intrigue: The Hidden Inner Circle of the Global Illuminati Conspiracy

Dark Majesty: The Secret Brotherhood and the Magic of a Thousand Points of Light

Millennium: Peace, Promises, and the Day They Take Our Money Away

New Age Cults and Religions

Mystery Mark of the New Age: Satan's Design for World Domination

Dark Secrets of the New Age

OTHER BOOKS BY RIVERCREST PUBLISHING

Behind Communism, *by Frank L. Britton*

Bohemian Grove: Cult of Conspiracy, *by Mike Hanson*

Gods of the Lodge, *by Reginald Haupt*

Letters on Freemasonry—The Classic, *by John Quincy Adams*

Matrix of Gog: From the Land of Magog Came the Khazars to Destroy and Plunder, *by Daniel Patrick*

New Age Lies to Women, *by Wanda Marrs*

Synagogue of Satan, *by Andrew Carrington Hitchcock*

FOR MORE INFORMATION

For a complete catalog of books, tapes, and videos about the Illuminati, secret societies, occultism, Bible prophecy, conspiracy and related topics, and for a free sample of the informative newsletter, *Power of Prophecy*, please phone toll-free 1-800-234-9673, or write to: RiverCrest Publishing, 4819 R.O. Drive, Suite 102, Spicewood, Texas 78669. For additional information we highly recommend the following website:

www.powerofprophecy.com

TABLE OF Contents

Dedicated to all the

unfortunate victims of

psychopath monsters in a

world gone mad.

The Psychopaths Are at the Threshold

"Some men are of so cruel a nature as to take a delight in killing men more than you should kill a bird."
— Thomas Hobbes

You will find *Psychopaths* to be a most unusual book. It is also a very necessary book. Reading it and studying its important implications may well save your life, and contribute to the salvation of many thousands — perhaps even *millions* — of *others*. This is not an exaggeration. *It is a dire warning*.

Psychopaths — criminal deviants — are at this very moment to be found at the highest level of our society. They have gained control of our universities and our public school systems. They have a firm grip on entertainment, dictating our musical tastes, movies, and television. Their minions watch over us constantly through our computers on social media. They use social media, movies, televisions and digital games to program and dictate the thoughts and behavior of our children. The psychopaths are in control of our news media — print newspapers, and their propaganda permeates the book industry.

The greatest achievement, however, of the psychopaths is their almost complete takeover of our federal, state, and local governments. What has been called the *Deep State* and its global appendages has seized power in our federal Congress, inside the executive branch (the Presidency), and even the Judiciary. Its chief proponents are inside our state houses and they have a firm grip on our local governments and school boards. They have been able, via manipulation, deceit, and lies to convince the majority of the population to abandon its traditional values and adopt alien ideas and immoral practices more useful to the rule of the psychopaths.

Still, their deviant control is *not* yet complete. Many in the body of politics are now awake and are actively opposing the psychopaths. These evil legions of predators are at the threshold of attaining nightmarish, total power over us. But opposition is rising.

When psychopaths control and influence our governmental system and dominate virtually every facet of our cultural existence, it can truly be said that the United States is a psychopathological society. But we are not yet a fully *Psychopath Nation*. The totalitarians are among us. They are rapidly spreading their seeds of mental disease everywhere, and all logical and sane human beings are astonished at their octopus-like movement surging virtually in every area of our lives. But we are not defeated. There is hope. America still has strategic assets we can use to stave off the psychological demons at our doorsteps. We will discuss these assets and their employment in this book.

You may be asking why I write this book, what my goals are in exposing the psychopathic element that now endangers America and intends to overthrow our Constitution and rearrange our daily lives. There are perhaps, many people more qualified to write this book and I pray those others will add to the materials I present here. For now, however, I am the only one that I know of to tackle this momentous issue.

Understanding History, Politics, and Psychology

To truly understand the emerging *Psychopath Nation* and to comprehend its gravity, takes special knowledge of the fields of history, politics, and psychology. These three fields essentially merge together and if we fail to take any of the three into account we remain inadequate and ill-equipped, unable to adjudge the dangerous shape of modern events and of human nature. Given this deficit, we find ourselves besieged with individual facts but unable to discern the full pattern of events that confront us. Indeed, we soon will find ourselves submerged in a sea of trivial minutiae while overlooking a volcanic eruption about to consume us.

I have always been fascinated with history and the development of human civilization, and much of my personal reading and study has been devoted to history. Political history has especially absorbed my mental energies. I received a BA Degree, *Summa Cum Laude* while at Park University in Missouri where I concentrated on the fourth branch of government, the Bureaucracy. I also studied psychology as it applied to communist political systems. At Park, I was awarded the *Phi Beta Kappa* citation for distinguished writing and the *Outstanding Political Science Graduate* award.

While earning my degree, I chanced to find in the dusty shelves of the university library a rare and little studied book by Dr. Harold D. Lasswell entitled *Psychopathology and Politics*. Published in 1930, I believe this is the first book to examine the psychological typologies found among politicians. Rather than reviewing the static structure of political systems, Lasswell looked at the personalities of politicians and grouped them into types, such as *Political Agitators, Political Administrators*, and so forth.

Lasswell believed that the study and analysis of the "private worlds" of political actors was extremely important, even essential to the understanding of political behavior. Personality, he theorized, dictates both the structure of government and policy.

Lasswell's work, though limited by his *Freudian* understanding, is considered a classic by some political scientists today. Lasswell was at the time of his book's publication a Professor of Political Science at the University of Chicago and his use of clinical psychology in the study of political science and government was a key pioneering effort.

Among Lasswell's astute observations are the following:

- Political Science without biography of individual leaders is merely a lackluster, static form of taxidermy.

- Political man utilizes his private interest in his carrying out of public interests.

- Political movements derive their vitality from the private interests of key leaders.

- Political crises are complicated by the activation of the primitive impulses of key leaders.

- Political symbols are particularly well-suited to effect political change because of their general circulation and emotive ability.

My Understanding Enhanced by Studies in Political Science and Psychology

My studies on communism, its theory and practice in government, while in the U.S. Air Force and at Park University, aided me in my current research on psychopathy.

A paper I wrote in 1971 at Park University, titled *Will the Communist Government in the Soviet Union Survive Until 1984?*, theorized that the psychopathic elite (Lenin, Trotsky, Stalin, *et al*) that had seized the reins of government in 1917 and terrorized the Soviet people was psychologically diminished and physically spent. It was, I stated, spinning out of control, and would be dissolved and replaced by 1984. My prediction came true with the advent of the Bush-Gorbachev New World Order.

Later, at North Carolina State University, I earned a Masters Degree in Adult and Community College Education, with additional study in social psychology, learning psychology, and developmental psychology.

At the University of Texas at Austin, where I was on the faculty for five years, I lectured on the contemporary military in society, studied the biographies of military leaders and focused on the possibility of world war. On the faculty of two other universities, I taught *Introduction to Political Science* and *American Government* as well as a senior-level psychology course, *Crises in Adult Adjustment*.

The study of psychopaths and their strange and peculiar role in human organizations fascinated me, and my work at North Carolina University, the University of Texas and other institutions increased my desire to learn more about what motivates these malicious individuals who are so destructive to society.

Political Psychopaths Begin to be Analyzed

Lasswell and his contemporaries in the 1920s and 1930s knew little about modern psychopathic science. They mostly debated the effects of Freud, Jung, and other psychiatric researchers. But the regimes of Hitler, Mussolini, Tojo, Lenin, Stalin, Roosevelt, and Churchill, and the elitist influences of the super-rich (Rothschild, Astor, Morgenthau, *et al*) were looming on the horizon. The causes of great human tragedies, misery, and suffering occurring in the 20th century were omitted from consideration. The most horrible psychopaths in human history evaded analysis.

In 1941 psychiatrist Hervey Cleckley's mind-catching book, *The Mask of Sanity: An*

Attempt to Clarify Some Issues About the So-Called Psychopathic Personality came out. It greatly popularized the study of psychopathic personalities. Cleckley, a medical doctor and psychiatrist, put to rest the widely held idea that all men are basically good, that all have redeeming qualities and can be rehabilitated and made useful to society.

Cleckley suggested that certain people are chronically evil. Such people possess only superficial qualities and are innately wicked. Cleckley identified this category as "psychopaths" and the term caught on. Today, *psychopath* is commonly used and the sociopath is considered a form of psychopathy. The two terms, psychopath and sociopath, are today interchangable.

Cleckley's work, *The Mask of Sanity*, was followed by a most important book by Canada's Dr. Robert D. Hare, *Without Conscience: The Disturbing World of the Psychopaths Among Us* (1993). Hare went one step further than Cleckley, giving us a scientific method of assessing whether a person is, indeed, a psychopath. Hare, who specialized in the study of prison inmates, developed a clinical test, the *Hare Psychopathy Checklist*, which is in common use today. It reveals the persons who are psychopaths with amazing accuracy, based on twenty psychopathic characteristics. Of course, its correctness is based on the qualifications and judgement of the psychologist or psychiatrist administering the test.

Briefly stated, according to Hare, *"Psychopathy is a personality disorder of persons without conscience and incapable of empathy, guilt, or loyalty to anyone but themselves."*

The insightful works of men like Cleckley and Hare are excellent resources for understanding the predatory species known as psychopaths. But neither they nor Dr. Lasswell's 1930 primer, *Psychopathology and Politics*, gave readers the keys to understand the depth of psychopathic activity as practiced on a *geopolitical* scale. Only Lasswell's study looked at the political leaders on a psychological level, and in his book, the science of psychopathy is not actively considered or even recognized for its geopolitical implications.

Psychopathy in a Nation or Nations

It was a book by a then unknown psychiatrist, Andrew M. Lobaczewski, a Polish dissident, entitled *Political Ponerology: A Science on the Nature of Evil Adjusted for Political Purposes*, published by Red Pill Press, in Canada, that really got my attention. Lobaczewski first published his book in Poland in 1984 and it was later published in America in 2006. It is a masterful study of the Communist psychopathic disease that gripped Poland, Eastern Europe, and much of the world in the 20th century.

As Lobaczewski proves, there are many psychological lessons to be learned about how the psychopaths took control of these nations and went on to subject entire populations to socialist imprisonment, torture, and death. Reading this book gives one a terrifying view of the historical calamities that overtook much of Europe and Asia and the predatory horror that is now descending on the United States and Europe. We will review some of Dr. Lobaczewski's findings later in this book.

The Focus of Psychopaths: Yesterday, Today, and Tomorrow

We have all seen the movies, television programs, and read about serial killers. We are aghast at the true stories of mental deviants like Jeffrey Dahmer, homosexual killer and cannibal who murdered over a dozen young victims. Our minds grow foggy contemplating the many women torturously slain by Ted Bundy, the youths savagely killed by John Wayne Gacy and buried under his house, or the women and children massacred unmercifully at the bloody hands of Henry Lee Lucas.

These inhumane monsters get our rapt attention because they have personally slaughtered multiple persons — three, five, fifteen, even as many as a hundred or more. Our minds boggle at their foul deeds and simply cannot fathom what inordinate emotions they possessed.

This book, however, is different. It surveys men and women who are just as sick and disturbed as the losers we so often adjudge to be serial killers, but are, in addition, able to deceptively work and manipulate their way to the top ranks of human society. These are the monstrous *mass killers* — people who have the unique ability, or the resources, to become the leaders of nations — Presidents, Prime Ministers, cabinet secretaries, agency heads, military brass, Senators, Congressmen, Governors, high judges, etc.

Such men — and women — hold the destinies of entire nations, or groups of nations (e.g. the European Community, the United Nations) in their hands. Whereas a Boston Strangler, a Green River Killer, a Ted Bundy, or a Jeffrey Dahmer may kill dozens, the mass serial killer is sometimes capable of murdering *millions* of innocents, through wars, starvation, disease, imprisonments, and other weapons and techniques of mass destruction.

By employing effective propaganda and unleashing human beings who are not actually psychopaths but are, shall we say, *proto-psychopaths,* or *semi-psychopaths*, they often rouse large populations (cities, mobs, cults, tribes, parties, organizations, etc.) to follow their psychopathic styles of behavior. These masses would otherwise not be psychologically stirred up nor would they be capable of such horrific and brutal acts of bloodshed and pain.

Consider that Hitler had his Brown Shirts, Stalin his Communist Youth, and Mao his revolutionary Red Guard. Not all members of such slavish disciple groups are psychopaths but many, nevertheless, are inspired and motivated by psychopathic leaders to act out their criminal activity.

Followers of psychopathic leaders often claim ideological reasons for their crimes, but, in fact, it is their own weak personalities and the hypnotically strong personalities of the deranged psychopathic leaders that guide their actions.

Caught up in a psychopathic fever or craze, ordinary people often do incredible things. They are moved to beat, kill, and maim, or to eagerly serve as concentration camp guards, while under the spell of psychopath leaders, Later, after the spell has lapsed they awaken and perhaps exclaim, "Why did I do that? What was wrong with me?"

Some express that, "A demon took hold of me." And that is exactly what psychopaths are — inhuman, predatory demons. Extraordinary beings, unlike anyone who has a human conscience and feelings. To fall under their hypnotic sway can result in tragic consequences. Even good men can literally become beasts.

— Texe Marrs
Austin, Texas

Chapter One

Soul Eaters

Soul Eaters: Belief in soul eaters is related to traditional folk beliefs in witchcraft, zombies, werewolves, and other cannibalistic spirited creatures. The soul eater is said to be able to devour a human's soul, causing a terrible wasting disease that can be fatal.

I have intensely studied the field of *psychopathy* for almost a half century. I have also met a number of *psychopaths* in my life, carefully observing their odd and unusual behavior and the malignant effect their behavior has on the people the psychopaths encounter. My lifelong preoccupation with psychopaths leads me to offer the following advice to you, the reader, regarding psychopaths whom you encounter in your life, whether that psychopath is a lover, a supposed friend, a boss, a co-worker, a neighbor, or even a member of your family. Here's my advice:

Flee! Do so now, immediately. And in the future, have absolutely nothing to do with him or her... or it!

What's more, regarding the psychopath:

Do not hate him.

Do not be angry with him.

Do not try to get revenge over him.

Do not attempt to get even with him.

Do not try to rehabilitate, cure, or change him.

This advice, which I will explain presently, seems extreme, but believe me, it is effective and, as you will discover later in the pages of this book, it may well prove to be life-saving. It will spare you much grief and avoidance of emotional and physical pain. Most of all, abandoning the psychopath and going on with your life will, no doubt, soothe your soul, leaving it free and clear of unbearable roadblocks and hindrances.

It has been said that a psychopath is nothing less than a ghoulish *soul eater*. A soul eater is a mythical creature in which many native peoples and tribes in Africa and the Caribbean regions believe. Movies and television have adopted these beastly shadow beings. They are said to be controlled by witchdoctors and to attack and take possession of human beings, bringing destruction of mind and consuming their victims' bodies, which waste away to oblivion. I believe that "soul eater" is a fitting description of these inhuman creatures who plague so many today.

Psychopaths Kill the Soul

Swedish author Juri Lina, in his perceptive book, *Architects of Deception*, states that non-psychopathic people, the normal, possess souls. They seek the truth. For this reason, he says, the deranged of society despise teachings that represent goodness and spiritual development. The psychopath is, therefore, particularly adept at murdering the soul.

"They consider it more beneficial to murder the soul rather than the body," Lina writes. They are after our souls. He quotes the noted French author and historian, Romain Rolland who wisely noted, "The murderers of the soul are the worst."

It was Jesus Christ who, in the Gospels, advised, "Fear not he who can kill the body. Instead, fear he who can kill both the body and the soul."

Spotting the Psychopath

Maybe you have encountered psychopaths in your life. Quite possibly, you know one or more such dull but manipulative creatures today. Certainly you will come into close contact in the future with one, five, or even more psychopaths. This book will help you spot deceptive psychopaths and identify them as such.

Such skills of identifying psychopaths are vital today, in our age when psychopaths are rapidly proliferating in number. There is a reason for this increase, which we will later discuss.

The psychopath does not burst forth with a business card that announces his presence. However, I am persuaded that the information herein will properly inform you and provide you with the insight and tools you can use to recognize and to refrain from an active association with psychopaths, as well as their "partners" and "associates," which I will call here, for our purposes, "proto-psychopaths." A proto-psychopath is a man or woman (or a transgender) who has attached himself to a *spellbinding* psychopath. Proto-psychopaths are useful to the psychopath in obediently carrying out various wicked deeds. Often, but not always, the proto-psychopath is a woman, a mate, of the psychopath. Proto-psychopaths are not usually full psychopaths. They are loyal followers.

Diagnostic Manual Omits Psychopaths

Although there is a lengthy psychiatric diagnostic manual to help psychiatric personnel evaluate patients and determine their particular mental illness, the current diagnostic manual does *not* cover the psychopath. He or she would probably fall into the disease category of *anti-social personality disorder*. This is an interesting oversight on the part of psychiatrists and is one reason for this book. It is absolutely essential that the reader study the characteristics and behavior of the psychopath's personality. *I am convinced that millions of lives are at stake.*

Sadly, many psychiatrists, psychologists, and psychotherapists are woefully deficient in diagnosing mental patients. Some years ago, Professor David L. Rosenhan, a Stanford University psychiatrist and attorney, conducted an experiment to judge the accuracy of the best mental hospitals in determining who is sane and who is insane.

Rosenhan and seven other psychiatric investigators arranged for themselves to be secretly committed to mental hospitals as severely disabled schizophrenic patients. They did not, however, disclose that they were "psuedo-patients." Yet the hospitals that they were investigating acted normally.

Amazingly, all eight of these people were found to be insane by hospital professionals. At the same time, Dr. Rosenhan says that it was quite common for actual psychiatric patients who resided at the hospitals to *correctly identify* the impostors as "sane."

"The fact that other patients recognized normality when staff did not raises important questions," said Rosenhan.

Eventually, at the conclusion of the test period, all eight impostors were discharged from the hospitals. At the time of their discharges, all were adjudged to continue as mentally ill schizophrenics despite their best efforts to convince the hospital staff of their sanity.

Serial Killers and Satanic Rituals

Imagine, now, a similar situation with psychopaths. It is thought that some five percent of all people are born psychopaths. Meanwhile, at least twenty percent (some claim up to fifty percent) of the entire prison population in the United States is psychopathic. How many are today misdiagnosed, even by experienced therapists? How, then, do we go about spotting these strange and dangerous deviants?

One way, of course, is to evaluate the psychopath by the types of crimes and criminal activities in which they engage. We can certainly all agree that serial killers and those who participate in horrific satanic rituals are inevitably psychopaths. David Berkowitz, the infamous serial killer from New York known as the "Son of Sam," confessed in a letter that he was part of an organized satanic group involved in ritual human sacrifice. He wrote:

> "Satanists (genuine ones) are peculiar people. They aren't ignorant peasants or semi-literate natives. Rather, their ranks are filled with doctors, lawyers, businessmen, and basically highly responsible citizens... they are not a careless group who are apt to make mistakes. But they are bonded together by a common need and desire to cause havoc in society. It was Aleister Crowley who said: 'I want blasphemy, murder, rape, revolution, anything bad'."

It is my finding that every psychopath hates God and loves himself. He is an atheist and a narcissist. It is true, also, that some psychopaths on death row, or to deceive a Parole Board, will have a "Christian conversion." They believe that by so doing they can persuade authorities to spare their lives or to grant early parole.

On the other hand, there are also psychopaths, like serial killer John Wayne Gacy, who, at his execution, was asked if he had any last words. He responded, "Kiss my ass."

Chapter Two

The Psychopaths are Everywhere

"It seems that psychopathic killers treat their victims like trash—to be used, abused, raped, tortured then killed and disposed of like garbage. They treat their victims with as much compassion as swatting a fly. There is no remorse at all."

—Victoria Redstall
Serial Killers—Up Close and Very Personal

Because of the sadistic historical record of satanic cults, we can easily surmise that many, if not most, Satanists are certifiable as psychopaths. But the astonishing truth is that psychopaths are everywhere around us. Martha Stout, a child psychologist on the faculty of Harvard Medical School, has written a valuable book, *The Sociopath Next Door* (sociopaths and psychopaths are synonymous) which makes this clear. Stout writes that psychopaths are not few and far between. On the contrary, they make up a significant portion of our population.

Any individual living in the world today will experience a relationship with, or know, at least one such person, in some capacity, during their lifetime. Actually, since about one out of every twenty persons is a psychopath, you and I can expect to come into contact with dozens—or hundreds—of psychopaths in our lifetime. Your banker, lawyer, teacher, or doctor could well be a conscienceless and incurable psychopath, as could your minister, your next-door neighbor, your husband or wife, or your child.

Politicians as Psychopaths

Some of your local politicians are inevitably psychopaths. Indeed, your congressman, senator, or perhaps even the President of the United States could well be a scheming and deceptive psychopath.

Almost all wars and armed conflicts are caused by psychopathic leaders. Yes, Hitler and Stalin were dangerous psychopaths, but their chief opponents in Washington, D.C. and London—Roosevelt and Churchill—were no doubt evil psychopaths as well. We can also review more recent times, up to the 21st century and we will discover psychopaths like George W. Bush, Bill Clinton, and Barack Obama. Such evil characters have placed millions of innocents in precarious situations and hundreds of thousands have been slain and maimed due to the psychopathic lies foisted on an unsuspecting world by such extremely dangerous persons.

It is for this reason I write this book. It is wise for all of us to fear the psychopaths such as Jeffrey Dahmer, John Wayne Gacy, and Ted Bundy. But the greatest threat to America, and indeed the whole world, lies in the twisted predators in whom we have deposited our lives, our families, and our treasures. My hope is that the lessons in this book will guide us in the future so we can escape the clutches of the dastardly criminals in our nation's capital.

The Ten Professions with the Most Psychopaths

An interesting article in *Business Insider* attempted to pick the ten professions with the most psychopaths. The article noted that psychopaths are difficult to spot most of the time. "They're not the 'Jack the Ripper' caricature you see in films or read about in books," said the author. "Often, psychopaths appear normal, which makes them hard to identify."

The article went on to contend that psychopaths are often found in leadership positions because of their ruthlessness and charisma. Many leaders also display an "inflated, grandiose sense of themselves, and a knack for manipulating other people."

Here are the ten professions where *Business Insider* speculated you'll find the most psychopaths.

1. *Corporate CEO:* Psychopathic CEOs use havoc and chaos inside people and organizations. This enables them to rise to the top of the career ladder. Olivia Solon, writing in *The Guardian* newspaper, says that psychopathic CEO's are especially found in Silicon Valley, where a high proportion of psychopaths are known to create a "crazy at the wheel" environment. As a Silicon Valley CEO, you "have to convince other people. So they are mostly charismatic, charming and make you suspend the belief that something can't be done."

Silicon Valley types are also willing to "manipulate through deception." But when things go wrong, the psychopathic CEO tends to flip out and resort to bullying. At that point, their "mask of sanity falls off."

2. *Lawyers:* Lawyers often are schemers, deliberately deceive others, and are cold-hearted. Politicians mostly come from lawyer ranks. They make very adept psychopaths. Notice also that the vast majority of U.S. Congressmen and Senators are lawyers. And many are psychopaths.

3. *Media, TV or Radio:* Narcissism is one trait of psychopaths, and media personalities are often blessed with an abundance of it.

4. *Salesperson:* Shameless self-promotion, he's told to promote products and services. The inability to be a team player makes psychopaths excellent for this field.

5. *Surgeons and Doctors:* Medical doctors are said by many to be indifferent to suffering and pain. Of course, some are caring and thoughtful, but as the technology of health care increases and as doctors increasingly gravitate to monied positions, psychopathic doctors proliferate.

6. *Journalists:* The era of "fake news" promotes freewheeling liars in journalistic endeavors. Today, who can trust the liars that deal out the news? Surveys show that over 90% of top journalists in print and digital media and on television are liberals and progressives. Their many lies and hocus-pocus "facts" are legion. Many excel as psychopaths and con-men.

7. *Law Enforcement:* Today, you are either a "bad cop" or a "good cop." Most are in the "good" category and thank God for them. But bad cops are legion, too. The recent revelations of chicanery and dishonesty among the top officials of the FBI and Justice Department prove law enforcement is a great avenue for psychopaths.

8. *Clergy and Ministers:* Newer stories about corrupt and evil clergymen are published daily across America. Experts say that over eighty percent of all Catholic priests are wicked homosexuals and/or child molesters. Who can say that the percentage is lower among Protestants and Jews, and Moslem Imams have a particularly poor reputation. Wherever professional clergy gather psychopaths are known to congregate. My book, *Pastors and Churches Gone Wild!* (RiverCrest Publishers) profiles many.

9. *Civil Servants/Government Bureaucrats:* Our governments, federal, state, and local, are packed with rule-happy psychopaths chomping at the bit to deny citizens a permit, a license, or some other official document. The IRS is overflowing with hateful psychopaths, and other government agencies, from the Fish and Wildlife Service to the Highway Department, and the Environmental Agency, are overstocked with psychopaths who enjoy tormenting hapless citizens. Fortunately, we also have some very talented and service-friendly bureaucrats working in Civil Service. But, be warned!

10. *Chef:* *Business Insider* magazine positions *Chef* at number ten in identifying psychopaths. I do not agree with this high rating and can name a dozen other professions where psychopaths seem to be found. But then, I do not personally know many chefs. Perhaps the busy kitchen presents a chaotic situation where psychopaths thrive.

Where Have You Met Psychopaths?

This list gives you some things to think about, but I wouldn't give these professions great precedence in your own life. Think back… what of the psychopaths in your life? Remember that "Oh—so wonderful" boyfriend who suddenly turned into a monster and a stalker? What about the "Sunday School teacher from hell" who seemed wonderful until you discovered the many deceitful lies she spread about you? And there's the "con-artist" who almost convinced you to invest thousands in that "sure thing?" Or the new Pastor at church who gave such thoughtful sermons but suddenly absconded with thousands of dollars from church coffers and also sullied the reputations of six or seven women at church with whom he had secretly been having sexual relations?

As a U.S. Air Force officer for over 20 years, a college professor for some seven years, and the founder of a Christian ministry that has been active now for more than a quarter of a century, I could relate my own sad knowledge of experiences with many psychopaths, some of whom I only belatedly realized were psychopaths. Psychopaths show up in the most unusual places and they are difficult to identify.

If I could have known early on that some of these men and women were troublesome psychopaths, my life would certainly have been easier. I would have pulled out all stops to *stay away from* the psychopathic workers and con-artists and led a much more pleasant life. But sometimes, circumstances force us to associate with psychopaths. They end up as our supervisors at work, our "friends" at church, our neighbors, our lovers, our spouses, or even our children. Sometimes, life throws us a wrench, and we have to use it. It's the only one we have. But use it quick, and then throw it out of the toolbox. No reason to keep unuseful "tools" in your life.

Chapter Three

"To Serve Man" (The Twilight Zone)

Subject: "The metamorphosis is of a man, from being the ruler of a planet to being an ingredient in someone's soup."

In 1962 on CBS-TV, in a now-famous episode of the anthology series, *The Twilight Zone*, the story of visitation to the planet earth by the Kanamits, a strange race of aliens is chronicled. It seems that earth is beset by many international crises. Suddenly, the aliens (nine feet tall and 350 pounds, with a huge, bulbous head) land in their space ship. One of them speaks to the people of earth in a televised speech from the United Nations via telepathy. He announces that his race has come to earth to share its advanced technology, to end famine, put an end to the nuclear threat, and end war forever. He offers as a gift a book in the Kanamit language.

Excited cryptographers, led by a man named Chambers and his assistant, Patty, go to work decoding the strange book. They first determine that the book's title is *To Serve Man*. Patty and the others continue their attempt to decipher the book.

Meanwhile, the seemingly benevolent Kanamits do, in fact, keep their word. They disband the earth's armed forces, insuring peace everywhere, and they invite earth's men and women to visit their planet on the space ship, declaring the new world a paradise. Many hopeful humans decide to volunteer to go, including Chambers, the head cryptographer working to decipher the book.

The glorious day arrives for Chambers and others to take their excursion to the paradise planet of the Kanamits. But just as Chambers mounts the space ship's boarding stairs, a frightened

Patty runs toward the space ship. She is held back by a Kanamit guard but cries out, "Mr. Chambers, don't get on that ship! The rest of the book, *To Serve Man*, it's… it's a cookbook!" The horrified Chambers turns and attempts to run down the stairs, but a Kanamit blocks him. Too late, the stairs retract, and the space ship lifts off.

Inside the space ship, Chambers is led to his spartan quarters, where he finds only a cot. A voice offers him a meal, delivered through a small opening in the wall. At first he refuses it, but the Kanamit encourages him to eat, "to keep from losing weight."

At the end of the episode, from his spartan quarters and cot, a discouraged and mentally defeated Mr. Chambers stares at the camera and dejectedly says, "Sooner or later, all of us will be on the menu. All of us."

Psychopaths—A Different Race, Here on Earth "To Serve Us"

The story of the Kanamits is remarkably like that of the psychopath with, of course, some quite different parallels. The psychopath is, amazingly, nothing less than a different species. Unlike the Kanamits, he physically resembles the human species. One rarely can tell him apart from human beings. But, the psychopath *is* different, *radically different*. Looks are deceiving.

For one thing, scientists have discovered that on brain scans, the *amygdala*, in the front part of the brain, reacts differently in the psychopath than in that of normal humans. The amygdala is the processor of human emotions. It is activated when the individual thinks of indulging in *moral or immoral acts*. In the psychopath, the amygdala does not function well. The question of guilt, of immoral behavior, does not register. The psychopath can lie and commit crimes freely, *without guilt*.

Nor does *fear* intrude on the psychopath's mind. Thus, the psychopath possesses

Austin American-Statesman

Wednesday, October 1, 2014

B Metro & State

+ Business

News: metrodesk@statesman.com; 512-445-3851
Subscribe: statesman.com/subscribe

Poll: Texans' biggest worries are abortion, immigration, B3

NEW DETAILS FATAL STABBING CASE

Video: Killer said he felt no emotion

Raul Rodriguez Cortez told sister he 'snapped' in slaying their mother.

By Jazmine Ulloa
julloa@statesman.com

Needing answers, Rocio Rodriguez testified Tuesday, she visited her brother in January at the Travis County Jail, less than a year after he took their mother's life.

In a chilling video that captured that conversation, Raul Rodriguez Cortez sounded both calm and earnest when he told the teenage girl that

he had "snapped" and killed Maribel Cortez in cold blood. It had likely been his destiny, the 18-year-old said, urging her to learn to move on, as he had.

"Were you conscious of yourself?" she asked in the recording.

"Well, the thing is, you know, I just didn't feel anything," he said. "I wasn't angry. I wasn't mad. I didn't feel anything."

The evidence came on the first day of testimony in a sentencing hearing for Rodriguez Cortez, who pleaded guilty to murder last week in the April

Raul Rodriguez Cortez faces between five years and life in prison in the 2013 death of his mother.

2013 death of his mother and is appearing before Judge Cliff Brown for punishment. He faces between five years and life in prison.

Prosecutors Amy Meredith and Marc Chavez have not asked the judge for a definitive sentence, but in court Tuesday, they painted Ro-

driguez Cortez as a remorseless and dangerous young man who had support from his family and could have improved his mental health should he have desired.

But defense lawyer Jon Evans contended the teen had cared deeply about his siblings, had lacked proper mental health treatment and had a strained relationship with his father, who witnesses said had once kidnapped the children in 2011 and threatened to kill them.

Austin police have said Ro-

Stabbing continued on **B5**

limited fear. The only thing to keep him from committing abominable crimes, or from harming other people is his consideration that he might be caught and punished. Otherwise, he is free from worry and may, in fact, look toward committing such crimes and foul deeds against hapless victims with an evil, unemotional attitude.

Psychopaths have no *remorse* for their vile acts and deceitful lies. They are not sorry for their victims. Indeed, they often experience a powerful exhilaration. As one psychopath killer stated, "It made me feel superior, like a superman. The more she begged for mercy, the more I got turned on. It was as if a sexual energy was released. I couldn't wait to kill again."

Like the psychopath, the manipulative Kanamit species does not view his human victims as equals. They are nothing more than *food*. To process (that is to kill) the human is not immoral. The psychopath, like the Kanamit, feels no guilt and no remorse. He stalks his prey with no concern for their welfare, but only to satisfy his appetite. That his prey is frightened and alarmed means nothing, either to the Kanamit or to the psychopath.

The callous, cold attitude of the psychopath cannot be understood by the normal person. A targeted victim is astonished. He or she may think that he can win by using logic on the psychopath, or perhaps he reasons he can gain the sympathy of the psychopath. He is bewildered when this fails. This failure results because the victim is not communicating with a human being. The psychopath is a *predator*, a monster who often comes disguised as a human. It is as if he has stumbled on a snake, an unfeeling poisonous reptile along the path.

The psychopath may have first made the acquaintance of his victim as a charming partner, a caring lover, a generous benefactor, or a friend. He may appear as a successful investor or businessman (who, suddenly, later proves to be a con-man,) or a knowledgeable co-worker. (We will later examine just how the psychopath operates to win over his victims.) He may even give evidence of being a wonderful Christian, perhaps a Sunday School teacher or new pastor, or a reliable politician.

How Could He? . . .

But then, he strikes, often when you least expect it. You are surprised, startled, unbelieving. *"How could he . . .?"* you exclaim, *"not him!"*

Then you begin to understand who—or what—you have been dealing with: A predator, an unfeeling monster. Yes, a reptile. And your whole outlook on life changes rapidly.

Your experience with a psychopath can easily shake a person's confidence in his or her fellow man. You may at first doubt yourself and your judgment. This is especially so if you come from a naive, trusting and loving environment or if you have for all your life been entitled or coddled. Meeting up with another person who appears loving, kind, intelligent, and caring might easily win your approval.

"Wow! She really loves me," you might exclaim. "She's so interested in my past, in my family, in my likes and dislikes." You feel she's a perfect match. Maybe your friends agree, or your parents. "How lucky I am," you reason.

Remember, Though, the Kanamit. He Offers Paradise, But . . .

If he or she appears a financial maven, a smart and successful stock market type, you may be encouraged to invest money with the psychopath. If he or she is your live-in lover, you may make the mistake of giving him access to your bank accounts or other funds. Then, one day, the person you trusted is gone, skipped the state, or the country, and left you high and dry.

Your Marvelous New Partner

Some are lured in by handsome, romantic men (or beautiful women) who seem ideal partners. These charming newcomers sweep them off their feet in a whirlwind affair. Be very wary of partners who have no auto, who have no permanent home, and no roots, no family to whom they can introduce you.

Especially beware of those who declare they have the same tastes and likes you have in music, art, entertainment, and so forth. These are all signs of the psychopath, who changes his persona and becomes everything you have ever desired in a lover. Until he has bilked you out of your life savings or otherwise abandoned you.

And don't be surprised if the psychopath leaves you for someone of the opposite sex. Psychopaths are notorious for bedding with men, women, and even children. They usually have no boundaries. John Wayne Gacy was married to a woman but raped and killed many young boys.

Richard Speck, who savagely murdered seven young female nurses, in prison had sex with many males. He even had a sex change operation to develop female breasts. The psychopath is a sexual beast. So pity the man or woman with children who takes in the psychopath.

The psychopath feels no guilt in abandoning a victim, or in stealing her money, etc. This is what the psychopath is; this is the species of reptile the victim has met unexpectedly, to his dismay. Moan all you want. Complain, grow very angry, rail against the psychopath. It's *your* problem, not his. If he has not yet abandoned you, he will likely just look at you with contempt and accuse you of misunderstanding him, of being cruel and being a bad person. The psychopath *never* admits guilt. In fact, the psychopath will probably get a kick out of your anger and frustration. You, on the other hand, are a *loser*.

The Psychopath Specializes in Changing Personas

Remember, the psychopath is not a *real* person. It's all stagecraft, an act, a persona, and soon he'll be gone, off to greener pastures.

A psychopath can be male today, tomorrow a lesbian, a kind-hearted soul or an abusive and perverted maniac. He can be anything he wants: a U.S. Air Force officer, an Army Green Beret, an FBI or CIA agent, or the member of an important, big-name family. Read the story online of "Clark Rockefeller," who fooled thousands of gullible people into believing he was one of the super-wealthy Rockefeller clan. That is, until he was arrested for a double murder. Then, the public found out that "Clark Rockefeller" was... well, someone else. Indeed, when asked by a reporter who he was, he smiled and responded, "Who do you want me to be?"

True, there are police officers, professors, doctors, lawyers, clergymen, bankers, and other high-level professionals who are psychopaths. Dr. Robert Hare and Dr. Paul Babiak have even published a book, *Snakes in Suits*, warning of them. Some disguise their evil and plow straight ahead into their chosen career. But from what I

BREITBART

TEXAS SCHOOL SHOOTING SUSPECT 'WEIRDLY NONEMOTIONAL' AFTER CONFESSING TO MASSACRE

f   ✉ EMAIL   🔴 SHARE   🐦 TWEET

Galveston County

The 17-year-old suspect in the killing of ten people at Santa Fe high school in Texas has confessed, authorities say, but his motivation for the attack remains unclear.

Santa Fe High School junior Dimitrious Pagourtzis hid a shotgun and a pistol under his trenchcoat before opening fire in a first-period art class on Friday, according to an affidavit filed by police. The FBI announced Saturday that it had taken the lead in the joint investigation, at the request of local authorities.

"He gave a statement admitting to shooting multiple people inside the Santa Fe High School with the intent on killing people," the police affidavit said. "Dimitrios advised he did not shoot students he did like so he could have his story told." The attack ended when he walked out of a classroom and surrendered to police.

Authorities say Pagourtzis planned the killings, carried out with weapons owned by his father. Though Pagourtzis allegedly wrote about his intention to carry out the attack, no indication of his motivation has yet been released.

According to one of Pagourtzis's lawyers, the 17-year-old appears to be "disoriented," and said his mood varied from "very emotional," to "weirdly nonemotional."

"There are aspects of it he understands and there are aspects he doesn't understand," the lawyer added.

have seen and experienced, their banal evil, lack of compassion, and remorseless behavior will eventually come out. They can't help themselves. They *love* doing evil and they actually enjoy hurting people. Again, it's what they are. The psychopath *loves* no one. Not their wives, husbands, children, mother, or father. They are cold, unfeeling, and without conscience. The psychopath is born evil. He or she must practice and rehearse being good, which is done only to get ahead in the "normal" world.

They Cannot Be Cured or Rehabilitated

Do not think you can "cure" or rehabilitate the psychopath. All the psychotherapy and counseling in the world is fruitless. As Jesus said of Judas, "It would have been better if he were never born."

Hare, in his perceptive book, *Without Conscience*, explains:

> "Psychopaths are social predators who charm, manipulate, and ruthlessly plow their way through life, leaving a broad trail of broken hearts, shattered expectations, and empty wallets. Completely lacking in conscience and in feelings for others, they selfishly take what they want and do as they please, violating social norms and expectations without the slightest sense of guilt or regret. Their bewildered victims desperately ask, 'Who are these people? What makes them the way they are? How can we protect ourselves?'"

Surely, the do-gooder says, we can rehabilitate these people. Perhaps their mental disease is a result of their upbringing. Perhaps some terrible events occurred to them early in life. Maybe their psychopathy is caused by the lack of love tendered to them early-on. After all, the altruistic do-gooder claims, everyone has good in them. We must strive to bring out the good.

These are false hopes and often they lead to tragedy. Many a psychopath has undergone corrective "therapy" while in prison. Even before that, untold numbers of young psychopaths were brought as a youth to juvenile delinquent authorities, stood before sympathetic judges or given other special treatment by counselors or other civil authorities.

The fact is, psychopaths, as opposed to mentally ill individuals—schizoids, narcissistic bullies and so forth—almost always repeat their anti-social crimes. They are recidivists. As Dr. Hervey Cleckley, author of *The Mask of Sanity*, puts it, the psychopath remains a psychopath throughout life, challenging society and creating chaos and misery for others. But he does not *feel* for his victims. Instead, he contemptuously loathes and despises others. As Cleckley observes, "goodness, love, horror, and human have no actual meaning, no power to move him."

The psychopath feels only a selfish form of pity and disrespect for those of us who experience love or who are repelled by horror or tragedy. He, on the other hand, is free from what he considers our stupidity. To the psychopath, conscience is an impediment, an obstacle to be discounted and dismissed, a characteristic of the weak, the fool, and the knave.

Psychopaths Make Devious Politicians

Can you not understand, therefore, how the psychopath would be superior to the good person in the *political arena*? The corrupt politician is a Machiavellian. He has no real character, no ideology or philosophy that moves him. He quickly adopts whatever strategy and thought-system that gives him an advantage. His goal is to *win*, to gain an advantage, no matter the toll in human suffering or misery.

The psychopath is consistent in maintaining a winning hand for only a brief time. He may be left-wing, centrist, or right-wing, a Democrat, Republican, or Socialist, whatever works at the time. But he will adopt a *new persona* whenever circumstances change. Nevertheless, he will lie and insist he has not changed. "I am still the same," he will claim.

The psychopathic politician will shed false tears over the death of a single person but express no regret at all in manufacturing pretexts that result in tens of thousands being slaughtered in warfare.

Does any reasonable, sane person doubt that such amoral individuals are *devils*? I well understand that many people reject spiritual causes for such hideous behavior. But how can we otherwise explain people who so readily unleash the machinery of war, who so maliciously outfit thousands of young men and women in uniform, and send them forth to kill untold numbers of civilian innocents? Is this not the devil's doing?

The Kanamits, the otherworldly beings depicted in the poignant episode of *The Twilight Zone*, may or may not have been devils. But certainly, their lies and manipulation of human beings led to unbelievably horrible behavior. As Kanamits, their cannibalism was understandable. We human beings were, to them, nothing more than food, something to assuage their appetite. To real-life psychopaths we, as human beings, are also considered nothing more than food to appease their reptilian appetites. Each of us is to "be served."

Chapter Four

Meet the Psychopath:
15 Characteristics of Psychopaths

"A true psychopath, regardless of social status, race, or gender, has absolutely no conscience, remorse, guilt, or empathy, ever."
— Thomas Sheridan
Puzzling People: The Labyrinth of the Psychopath

I assume that in obtaining and reading this book, you sincerely want to understand the psychopath. You want to be able to identify him or her, and if at all possible, avoid him. So, I won't pull any punches. Let me get straight to the truth. The psychopath is a no-good, rotten, evil caricature of a person. Not a real person, of course, but a cold, toxic, soulless monster who resembles a person.

A person, even a mean, selfish, relatively loveless person, somewhere in the recesses of his mind, has feelings. He may be selfish and a narcissist, but he does feel some level of remorse. He has a conscience and he practices some type of morality and human emotion. But the psychopath has none of these things. He is a predator, a malicious force, constantly seeking mastery and control over every person he meets.

On a planetary level, the psychopath starts wars, employs machines that kill, rampages with his armies across national boundaries. On a personal, familiar level the psychopath viciously deceives victims, cons investors of savings, cheats consumers, leaves lovers heartbroken, and otherwise ruins lives. At whatever level he is able to attain, he damages innocents, and those who encounter him are often bewildered.

Jon Ronson, in his book, *The Psychopath Test*, warns that generally, "We're raised to believe that deep down everyone has a conscience." But then along comes the psychopath. "Everyone in the psychological field," said Ronson, "regards psychopaths as inhuman, relentlessly wicked forces, whirlwinds of malevolence, forever harming society."

Whether we are studying Joseph Stalin, mass killer of millions, or Bernie Madoff, Wall Street robber of thousands, every psychopath has similar tendencies and characteristics. Professor John Hare, a criminal psychologist, is perhaps the world's leading expert on psychopathy. Hare has developed a list of 20 criteria to determine if a person is of a psychopathic mind. The test is accurate and is today used by many other experts in this field. I employ a number of Hare's psychopathic traits, below, in my own list, but I add other important characteristics based on my own research and observations.

15 Characteristics of a Psychopath

It is important not to name someone a psychopath unless you have undeniable evidence. We do not want to stigmatize people who have perhaps one, two, or even three traits of the typical psychopath. In this book, I often state *my opinion* about particular individuals being psychopaths. I also explain *why* I believe that person is a psychopath. The individual may protest and probably will. An arrogant psychopath never admits he or she is a psychopath. After much careful thought and evaluation, I present to you below my 15 characteristics of the typical psychopath. I encourage you to refer to these characteristics when personally judging whether a person might be a psychopath.

Checklist: 15 Characteristics of Psychopaths

1. Lack of Empathy
2. Lack of Conscience
3. Lack of Remorse
4. Glib and Superficial
5. Double-minded
6. Deceitful and Manipulative
7. Grandiose Ego
8. Invented Personas
9. Failure to Accept Responsibility
10. Shallow Emotions
11. Poor Behavioral Controls
12. Parasitic Lifestyle
13. Power Seeker
14. Invokes Pity
15. Morally Debauched

Let's take a look at each of these characteristics.

1. Lack of Empathy

The most identifiable and most important character trait of the psychopath is his *lack of empathy*. Like robots and androids, they care nothing for the pain, suffering, and inconvenience they cause others. They see people as mere objects to be used, dominated, and then discarded. They do not "feel" another's pain or hurt.

MRIs of psychopaths indicate no response when pictures and videos are shown of people being severely injured in accidents. They do not register the psychopath's concern in seeing victims tortured or hurt. Blood and gore do not budge them.

Psychopaths often "pretend and make-believe" with others present when victims are injured, hurt, or tortured. There is not a spark of human kindness in the heart of psychopaths. We can recall the dead-pan words of President Bill Clinton when confronted with stories of tragedies: "I feel your pain." Pretend and make-believe. A psychopath finds it easy to cheat, swindle and defraud, looking upon his victim as a contemptible fool.

2. Lack of Conscience

The psychopath has no guilt. He commits crimes without any afterthought of sorrow. He has no regrets. He is a predator without barriers and often is a highly successful prosecuting attorney, lobbyist, and especially a politician. He enjoys getting away with crime and is adept at leaving "clues" with police. His deceit is a matter of pride. When confronted with evidence of a crime, he often gets angry and defiant. He will vociferously deny involvement or claim that the victim "asked for it," or "deserved what she got."

If his victim was raped, the psychopath might claim, "She wanted it. She was dressed like a slut," or "Why was she out so late at a bar?"

Bernie Madoff, convicted of sweeping investment crimes, rather than apologizing, snapped, "The whole world is a Ponzi scheme."

A psychopath who knifed and killed a bartender, commented, "He had it coming. He refused to give me another drink. He said I was drunk."

A psychopath who cruelly beat up his wife, responded, "She should have shut her mouth. She knew I was getting hot under the collar."

A psychopath who viciously assaulted a friend said, "He kept demanding I pay him back what I owed him. A mere $10.00. I finally kicked his ass. He deserved it. I was patient; finally, I just blew up."

3. Lack of Remorse

Having committed offenses and crimes, the psychopath shows no remorse. It is always telling during court to watch the accused make a statement during the penalty phase. Only if his clever attorney has properly instructed him will he know to make reference to the suffering of his victims. Nor will he apologize to the families and survivors. Often his statements are excuses and are self-serving.

This lack of remorse is a painful reminder to survivors and family members of what a cruel and callous member of society the psychopath is.

Mass political killers—like George W. Bush, Vladimir Lenin, Joseph Stalin, or Pol Pot—are not sorry about the people they kill. It's all just "collateral damage." The victims are not considered human.

4. Glib and Superficial

Psychopaths can be "big talkers," even witty and amusing. They often appear charming and likable, slick and smooth. Their talent enables the psychopath to easily deceive victims and fool chosen targets. On the other hand, their personalities are mercurial and the psychopath can switch "on a dime" and say something unwise and inappropriate.

5. Double-Minded

Double-mindedness is a primary characteristic of the psychopath. Every psychopath is possessed by this extraordinary trait. The Holy Bible says that, *"A double minded man is unstable in all his ways" (James 1:8).*

Doublethink was described by George Orwell in his novel, *1984*, as simultaneously holding two conflicting beliefs. Orwell describes it this way:

> "The power of holding two contradictory beliefs in one's mind simultaneously, and accepting both of them... To tell deliberate lies while genuinely believing in them, to forget any fact that has become inconvenient, and then, when it becomes necessary again, to draw it back from oblivion for just so long as it is needed, to deny the existence of objective reality and all the while to take account of the reality which one denies—all this is indispensably necessary. Even in using the word doublethink it is necessary to exercise doublethink. For by using the word one admits that one is tampering with reality; by a fresh act of doublethink one erases this knowledge; and so on indefinitely, with the lie always one leap ahead of the truth."

Thus, the psychopath contends that free speech is absolute, but there are some things you cannot say and will be punished for saying, even if they are true. The psychopath holds that everything has two opposite sides, but both sides are true at different times.

For the psychopath, gender and nationality are flexible and changeable. War is peace, freedom is slavery, and ignorance is strength. Only the simpleton would believe and confess otherwise, they say.

The psychopath believes in an ever-changing, non-absolutist world. Said the men who sparked the catastrophic French Revolution: "Everything must change." This is because "white equals black and black equals white." We are all citizens of "Never Never Land," but the normal person doesn't get it.

Here's how one psychopath, founder of the Church of Satan, Anton LaVey, explained it:

> "There are not always two sides to every issue. That statement is a ridiculous slogan. There is invariably another alternative, a THIRD SIDE, a satanic side."

You will run into great difficulty in attempting to debate a psychopath. He will always be contradictory and illogical and you will be frustrated. Quit and go on is my advice.

However, if it is your initial meeting with a psychopath, he will appear to be your great friend. He will pretend to care about you. He will have the same tastes in music, food, and clothing as you. He will love your political choices—they will be the same as his. If you are a potential lover, he will charm you. You will be the most beautiful woman or most the handsome man he/she has ever known, etc.

But once he has won you over, then the downgrading begins. He will have no use for you. You will be stupid, make terrible decisions, and be a worthless human being. After your self-confidence is at an all-time low, suddenly he will be gone. It's on to a new target. He has bled you dry, and he's through with you. Oh, yes. If possible, he'll take your possessions with him and empty your bank account.

6. Deceitful and Manipulative

The psychopath specializes in being deceitful and manipulative. After all, life is just a never-ending game for him. He goes through life searching for targets of deception and loves it when he comes across one. In deceiving, he exhibits his supposedly superior intelligence and proves once again that everybody *but him* is a fool, an unwitting dupe of deception.

The book, *1984*, is representative of what happens in a thoroughly deceitful and manipulative society. Big Brother's agents and politicians lied constantly and the populace was expected to change their perceptions to believe firmly in the current lie. Propaganda, Newspeak, and Doublespeak were ordinary companions of the deceived.

Politicians who are psychopathic are experts in deception and manipulation. Their wordplay twists men's minds. A concentration camp is a "reeducation center," or a "processing center," or even a "welcoming" place. Abortion is always "reproductive rights," or "pro-choice." Imprisonment and incarceration is "extraordinary renditions." Invasion or attack is a "surge." Conquest and occupation is "nation-building." Death or murder is "termination," etc. Orwellian language and weasel words are common to these individuals.

7. Grandiose Ego

Looking around his world, the psychopath sees only normal people who have empathy and feelings toward others, who have a conscience, who are remorseful when they lie, cheat, or steal. He has none of these human feelings and emotions and so he reasons that he is superior and a super-man. The others are weaklings.

The psychopath has a grossly inflated view of his self-worth and his abilities. He is often an arrogant person, a braggart. Everyone else is far behind in intelligence, good looks, wit, charm—or so he thinks. He is narcissistic. Police have noted that, on occasion, the criminal psychopath will confess a crime simply to prove how shrewd and cunning he is. Psychopaths don't believe in a God (except for themselves!), but sometimes will admit they would like to be God's adviser.

Political psychopaths can develop a large audience of gullible admirers who fall for their braggadocio and their ego-mania. Every high-level political psychopath has "groupies" who will follow him into a hot oven. Religious cult psychopaths have the same manic ability to spell-bind and sway an audience.

For example, Charles Manson had many women write to him and express their love and admiration. Richard Ramirez, the *Night Stalker*, who murdered numerous women, had a lengthy list of women admirers, and even serial murderer John Wayne Gacy carried on with a bevy of strange people who idolized his accomplishments.

8. Invented Personas

Psychopaths are found in many different career fields—lawyer, medical doctor, salesman, CEO, politician, etc. But rarely does the psychopath stay a lifetime in one career and if he does, you will find that he has other pursuits on the side. For example, John Wayne Gacy was a construction contractor and was also a part-time clown. Many psychopaths turn to gambling and, of course, most are philanderers and have many sex partners. Their side jobs suit the psychopath's need for excitement and his impulsiveness and provide covers for his nefarious activities and time missing.

However, a striking number of psychopaths have a lifetime of invented personas. They will go from target to target, changing personas, becoming different persons. Their resumé changes over and over. Often he will invent a new persona as he deceives and manipulates a victim, claiming to the victim he is a secret CIA agent or a high-level military officer or perhaps an undercover detective. The list of invented personas can grow and grow. And when he gets bored with that victim, or has used up all of the victim's money and resources, he moves on to his next target, once again changing personas.

It is not unusual to find several victims of the same psychopath who invents a quite different name and resumé for each. In the age of computer dating services, it becomes easy to go from victim to victim, deceiving each and acting as a different person. Some psychopaths deserve the title "Catfish" for this change artist's ability.

There are a number of documented cases of male and female psychopaths who pose as a member of distinguished families with impressive names. I referred earlier to "Clark Rockefeller," who bilked a large list of victims. Later, interviewed while under arrest, this particular psychopath was asked, "Who really are you?" The psychopath with the fake identity smiled broadly and replied, "Who do you want me to be?" It turned out that the psychopath had several aliases.

9. Failure to Accept Responsibility

The psychopath has a chronically unstable and aimless lifestyle. He is unreliable, breaks promises, and does not fulfill obligations and commitments. The term "shiftless" comes to mind. He is disloyal to friends, fails to make good on debts. He is, in a word, unprincipled.

10. Shallow Emotions

Human emotions such as love, care, and devotion have no part in the mental life of the psychopath. He has no feeling of empathy, no compassion, no pity, no morality, no romantic feelings, no patriotism, no sadness, no happiness. The psychopath is a cold, indifferent, superficial *monster*.

Psychopaths must put on masks so they can function in the world of normal people. They have no sympathy for the sick and ill who are hospitalized. They are never embarrassed, have little or no anxiety or fear. Psychopaths do not know when to cry at tragedy or celebrate a victory with friends. Some buy and read books to learn how to make emotional responses.

The psychopath who owns a pet—say a dog or cat—does not love the animal. It is merely a possession. He treats his wife (or husband) and children in the same manner—as possessions. And he can be quite brutal when and if his "possession" decides to leave him. He is liable to declare, "If I can't have you, no one will."

However, when the psychopath tires of his "possession," he is quick to jettison a wife, girlfriend, or perhaps a pet. In such a case, he has no emotional attachment.

11. Poor Behavioral Controls

Troublesome behavior at an early age is common among psychopaths. Cruelty to animals—and to other children—is one sign of a person's psychopathy. This cruelty begins at an early age. For example, as a boy, George W. Bush enjoyed putting firecrackers up a frog's backend and lighting them. Alberto de Salvo, the Boston Strangler, as a child, shot arrows at dogs and cats he had trapped; the two Columbine killers, Eric Harris and Dylan Klebold, mutilated and tortured animals for fun, and a young Jeff Dahmer killed dogs and cats and set up a pet cemetery where he also buried the bodies of stray animals such as squirrels and rabbits.

The psychopath is an evil person and his vicious nature in harming a brother or sister, or in torturing a helpless pet, is a big red flag to parents. Some parents attempt to justify this behavior, claiming the child is just "experimenting," or is "curious."

Vandalism, lying, cheating, stealing, and bullying are often employed by psychopaths. As teenagers, they take illegal drugs, crave horror movies, break curfew rules and otherwise frequently engage in unseemly conduct. As adults, this type of behavior leads to embezzlement, sexual improprieties and promiscuity.

Adult psychopaths have an affinity for criminal behavior. They are aggressive, their tempers flare, and the slightest provocation by others leads them to seek retribution and revenge. Social mores have little meaning to psychopaths.

Psychopaths are violent and abusive. Their violence and threat thereof are often calculated to intimidate and dominate victims. They are risk-takers and lawbreakers. The threat of punishment fails to deter them.

The cruelty of the criminal psychopath who kills has few boundaries. FBI agent, John Douglas, in his book, *The Anatomy of Motive*, writes:

> "These killers… enjoy killing… they are not insane… they enjoy the hurt they inflict and, in one case, when a (psychopathic) teenager forced caustic cleaning fluid down an 80-year-old woman's throat just to steal a few bucks, and she died in agony, the offender laughed."

Christopher Berry-Dee, in his frightening book, *Dead Man Talking*, interviewed 30 of the world's most heinous serial killers, all sexual psychopaths. He writes that their sickening tales of murder "are beyond the comprehension of normal people." He goes on to add:

> "These sexual psychopaths love to play mind games and often are as cunning as hyenas. They are control freaks who attempt to manipulate even a seasoned criminologist like me, prompting the chilling question: What chance did their vulnerable prey have against such twisted characters, who can appear as innocent as the man or woman next door."

12. Parasitic Lifestyle

Many psychopaths are leeches. They depend on others for their existence, for financial support, for rewards. We find that some in politics are parasites. For example, three recent presidents never really had an occupation other than politician—Bill Clinton, George W. Bush, and Barack Obama.

The parasitic psychopath will lie, con, manipulate, cheat, and blend in. He mimics other emotions, learning peoples' likes and dislikes and performing them as does an actor, pretending to be someone he is not to advance his own interests. He uses deceit and unscrupulous behavior to bleed others and take from them.

Some of these parasites use the internet to make romantic contacts and then feed their target lies and disinformation to persuade the target he is their ideal partner or soul mate. The psychopath becomes whoever his projected target wants him to be. He latches on to the deceived romantic partner until her money is gone and then moves on to a new target. These types of parasitic psychopaths are ever searching. They will go from partner to partner in a vain attempt to conquer and win. Some leave a long trail of broken hearts but they themselves suffer no personal loss. They are indifferent to the tragedy they sow.

13. Invoke Pity

Psychopaths are experts at invoking pity. This especially wins over people who are soft-hearted and believe they can help the poor, afflicted psychopath. Victimology is an art and science to the psychopath. He will tell you no one has ever suffered as much as him. His mother beat him, his brother or sister passed away, his boss at work doesn't appreciate his talents, etc.

If a psychopathic husband beats his wife, expect him to cry and wail, "I don't know why I did that. Please forgive me." The poor wife, even with bruises and a black eye, has pity and forgives. Then, of course, it happens again, and the sob story is repeated.

14. Power Seeker

Winning is everything for the psychopath. He is controlling and obsessed with getting his way. To lie and steal is acceptable in order to win. He prides himself on deceit and exploitation. He is a risk-taker who takes chances to vault ahead of his peers, and if he is vanquished or beaten, he degrades and criticizes the actual winner, claiming he cheated or fudged to win. He always has an excuse ready in the event he loses.

15. Morally Debauched

The psychopath is a moral reprobate. He is continually lying and is a manipulator. He has no sexual scruples at all and to win, he will have sex with either a man or a woman. He feels no love or compassion. He is continually on the lookout for new sexual conquests and relishes dealing in criminal activity.

As a politician, the morally debauched psychopath excels, easily defrauding those who believe in him. Political party affiliation means nothing to the psychopath. He will bend his ideology and political vices to fit. He is a Machiavellian character, not to be trusted, turning on opponents and friends alike as circumstances dictate.

Advice to the Reader:

This checklist of 15 characteristics, or traits, of the psychopath should be closely applied when determining whether a person is a psychopath. Some psychopaths possess all 15, others only eight or nine. But here is my advice to the reader:

1. Be very careful when applying a characteristic to a particular person. Unless you are a psychiatrist or an individual qualified to evaluate psychopathic behavior, you might make a serious mistake in judging one's personality. If you must, discuss your findings with a professional therapist.

2. I have developed this list after some fifty years of personal observation of psychopaths and after much professional study and reading. Others in this field may agree with these observations. The exceptional book, *Without Conscience: The Disturbing World of the Psychopaths Among Us*, by Dr. Robert Hare, has its own list of characteristics. If you are interested, I encourage you to obtain Hare's excellent book.

3. Never tell a psychopath he or she is a psychopath, and never use my checklist of characteristics to prove your point. The psychopath will never admit he is a psychopath, and you will only rile him or her up. The psychopath is very adept at causing others to believe that *you* are psychologically unstable, that you are to blame for the difference between you and him. He is often able to deceive even the best of counselors and therapists.

One other point: If you are worried, or convinced, that you are a psychopath yourself, then be assured that you are *not* a psychopath. If you were, you would not be asking the question. Every person, to some degree, possesses one or more of my 15 characteristics. We are all subject to human weaknesses and temptations. However, if many or most of the characteristics apply to you, then… seek a professional opinion.

Chapter Five

Trump Derangement Syndrome — A Prelude to National Psychopathy

Definition: *Trump Derangement Syndrome* is a term for the mental disorder of Trump opponents who are so irrational and psychologically disturbed they are incapable of accurately perceiving the world, interpreting every Trump action as evil and worthy only of contempt.

The United States has long been a nation in which the majority of people accepted the decisions of voters and voluntarily agreed to give the winning candidate credit for the victory. The new President, for example, is accepted by the voters as the legitimate office holder and even afforded a "honeymoon" period in which to promote his policies.

But in the case of Donald Trump, no such "honeymoon" period was offered. Even after the election and before the inauguration, many Democrats and certain "Rhino" Republicans (actually liberals) so hated Trump that they refused to view him as the

A Hillary Clinton supporter melts down and screams at the sky. This behavior was common on election night, 2016.

legitimate winner. Instead, their hero worship of Democrat loser Hillary Clinton and their hatred of Trump's campaign promises caused a huge number of people to literally suffer mental melt-downs. On November 8, 2016, election night, as the results rolled in and it became apparent that Trump was the winner, crowds of Hillary supporters gathered together to weep and moan. Some held up their arms and shouted obscenities. Others collapsed in tears, while still others raised their heads and shouted aloud, like a bunch of loons. Even some media news personalities wept and bemoaned the fact that their idol, Hillary, had lost.

Hillary Clinton reportedly went to her hotel room, emotionally reacting to the loss, cursing and shouting. She refused to publicly concede defeat, traditional for defeated candidates, abandoning a throng of her supporters in the auditorium. Most were in a state of disbelief. After all, the opinion polls had Hillary Clinton ahead from 7 to 11 points.

At Donald Trump's inauguration ceremony, sixty Democratic Congressmen refused to attend.

In the ensuing days, the mental malaise grew stronger, as Democrats and the media (which is overwhelmingly Democrat and progressive, or liberal) continued to rage and demonstrate their displeasure. Celebrities in Hollywood, on Broadway and in the entertainment industry were especially angry and affected.

The malaise gained such strength that psychologists and others were forced to adopt a name for what many perceived as a legitimate mental disorder. At first it was called "Trump Anxiety Disorder," then "Trump Psychosis." Finally, the term "Trump Derangement Syndrome" came into vogue. So today, those people possessing an inordinate hatred or an unnatural distaste for everything Donald Trump says and does are deemed to be afflicted with *Trump Derangement Syndrome (TDS)*.

People with TDS are so filled with hatred and/or distrust of the President that nothing he does pleases them. They are virtually 100% opposed to his policies and agenda, even to his physical characteristics (many call him the "orange man" or "Mr. Cheeto," referring, of course, to his complexion).

TDS victims are dismissive and contemptuous and are acutely beset with Trump paranoia. General hysteria often prevails and victims show signs of psychic pathology. Their hatred is so intense and they are so unhinged that their critical judgement is hopelessly impaired.

President Trumps's policies are universally portrayed by people with TDS as dangerous and must, they reason, be vigorously attacked. In effect they suffer from a spasm of self-delusion.

People with TDS are practically everywhere, and as celebrities and media personalities, many are able to garner a lot of publicity. For example, all the news hosts of *CNN, MSNBC*, and *ABC* are affected, as are numerous TV and Movie Stars and radio hosts. Their ranks include: *MSNBC's* Joe Scarborough and Mika Brzezinski, actresses Alyssa Milano, Bette Midler, Barbara Streisand, Ashley Judd and Meryl Streep; TV stars Chelsea Handler and Samantha Bee; actors Robert DeNiro and Jim Carrey; producers Rob Reiner and Michael Moore, Democratic politicians, Congressmen Nancy Pelosi, Maxine Waters, and Jerry Nadler; recording artists like Snoop Dog, John Legend, Beyoncé, Madonna and Taylor Swift.

Also, many people who are supporters of globalism and opposed to nationalism and to "America First" philosophies are known to have Trump Derangement Syndrome (President Trump announced in a United Nations speech on September 24, 2019, "Globalism is dead!").

Likewise, bureaucrats and members of the reputed, infamous "Deep State" White House have been charged with crimes, fired or otherwise terminated. These have joined the many TDS afflicted—people such as former FBI Director James Comey, Asst. FBI Director Andrew McCabe, etc.

So the list of people afflicted with TDS goes on and on.

A prominent symptom evident in almost every person suffering from TDS is profanity. Curse words (especially "f__ Trump") are commonly spouted. America has never—I repeat, never—experienced such a widespread display of foul mouth,

Entertainer Madonna gave a speech before a large crowd and said she has been thinking about "blowing up the White House."

Congresswoman Maxine Waters (D-CA) told an excited mob of listeners to go out into their communities where they should confront Trump supporters, at restaurants, department stores, even service stations. "Tell them they are not wanted anywhere," she ranted.

Actor Robert DeNiro receives a kiss from actress Meryl Streep after giving a looney-tunes speech in which he cursed Donald Trump and threatened to punch the President.

Whoopi Goldberg is definitely afflicted with what many term, Trump Derangement Syndrome.

angry words directed against the President of the United States.

TDS sufferers are known to make physical threats against President Trump, his administrative staff, and against anyone daring to wear a T-shirt or a ball cap with a message suggesting the wearer is a supporter of Donald Trump. Bad behavior and violence are often seen in TDS prone persons.

TDS sufferers demand impeachment of President Trump. He's been under a threat of impeachment since the day he was elected.

The question is: Is there really such a mental sickness category said to be Trump Derangement Syndrome, or is this just a passing fad of some maniacal variety? It is difficult to go back in history and find a mental illness so affecting political losers like Trump Derangement Syndrome.

Certainly, TDS is not listed in the Psychiatrist's Diagnostic Manual. But then, it is true that even the formally listed categories of illnesses are disputed by psychiatrists and psychologists. Indeed, researchers admit that psychiatric diagnoses are "scientifically meaningless" in treating mental health. In a study published in 2019, (published in the scientific journal, *Psychiatry Research*) it was stated that such illnesses as bipolar disorder, schizophrenia, depression, anxiety, and trauma-related disorders overlap each other in individuals. Psychiatric diagnoses often vary considerably. What to one specialist is a bipolar disorder, to another specialist is viewed as schizophrenia, for example. Such diagnoses tell us little about individual patients.

One notes that the significant mental sickness described elsewhere in this book as *Psychopath* is not even found in the Psychiatric Diagnostic Manual. That is why I include in chapter four a list of 15 characteristics of the psychopath to enable you to make your own evaluation of disturbed individuals.

Still, a growing number of psychiatric specialists are now known to diagnose individuals as suffering Trump Derangement Syndrome.

I ask the question, however, are those disturbed people *also* psychopaths? In fact, some *are* psychopaths, but many, if not most, are not. They simply do not meet the criteria to be regarded as psychopaths, not possessing a significant number of psychopathic characteristics.

Instead, many with TDS are simply grossly immature, some are narcissistic, and others are elitist, thuggish, or selfish. These are negative traits to be sure, but do not necessarily land such individuals in the umbrella of psychopathy.

The strange contagion of Trump Derangement Syndrome seems to be a part of the rise of the inevitable *Crazy Times* era prevalent in a nation on the threshold of moving into Psychopath Nation status. It is frightening proof that many are falling prey to the psychopaths and are afflicted with the advanced stages of *proto-psychopathy*. America may not have much time to spare. We should all be watching out for the horrific, bloody Rise of the Psychopaths.

Photographic Proof of Trump Derangement Syndrome

In the following pages, proof is presented evidencing the meteoric rise of Trump Derangement Syndrome.

Greta Thunberg, an angry 16-year old from Sweden, was reportedly paid by globalist George Soros to come to the United States, where she gave a pro-climate change speech and literally threatened her polite audience.

Svante Thunberg   Malena Ernman   Greta Thunberg

Greta and her parents are activists tied to Antifa, a progressive terrorist group.

WATCH: CHELSEA HANDLER ADMITS TRUMP'S ELECTION DROVE HER TO SEEK PSYCHIATRIC HELP AND DRUGS

| f 78,673 | ✉ EMAIL | 👍 SHARE | 🐦 TWEET |

ChelseaHandler instagram crop

Instagram/chelseahandler

Far-left comedienne Chelsea Handler admitted that the election of President Donald Trump forced her to seek psychiatric help and smoking cannabis for anxiety relief.

Appearing on *Real Time With Bill Maher*, Maher quizzed the failed Netflix talk show host about her new book *Life Will Be The Death of Me*, where she tells the story of how Trump's election victory over Hillary Clinton sent her spiraling toward a "mid-life identity crisis."

"Yeah I had a midlife identity crisis once Trump won, because I had never had my world feel so unhinged I think," Chelsea Handler explained. "And I had to pay a psychiatrist to listen to me bitch about Donald Trump for about the first three weeks."

"For me it was a huge emotional trigger of everything being destabilized and privileged I'd been all my life to be this upset every day... and the outrage and the anger, I just wanted to fucking fight people," she continued.

Maher then asked Handler about how Trump's election also led her towards drugs such as marijuana to help quell her political anxieties. Over recent years, Handler has made countless bizarre rants about Trump and his supporters, even questioning whether they enjoy watching people suffer.

"What I discovered is alcohol and outrage are not a good mix... so I pivoted to towards

RASHIDA TLAIB'S FIRST DAY IN CONGRESS: 'WE'RE GONNA IMPEACH THE MOTHERF**KER.'

47,409

by KYLE MORRIS | 3 Jan 2019 | 21,175

▶   🎧 LISTEN TO STORY   2:35

On her first day as a new member of the United States House of Representatives, Rashida Tlaib (D-MI) called on her colleagues to begin taking steps towards impeaching President Trump.

Tlaib was fetted at a raucous reception later in the day by left wing advocacy group MoveOn.org. Her closing remarks there were, "We're gonna impeach the motherfucker."

Dave Weigel
@daveweigel

Raucous reception for @RashidaTlaib at MoveOn reception near the Hill. Her closing remarks: "We're gonna impeach the motherfucker."

9,414   9:23 PM - Jan 3, 2019

2,630 people are talking about this

CNN's Kathy Griffin displaying the (simulated) decapitated head of President Trump, a sign of her dislike for his "America First" views.

A sign at a meeting of Trump haters depicting the President as Hitler.

SOAP STAR NANCY LEE GRAHN SMEARS IVANKA TRUMP AS A NAZI FOR GETTING A DOG

| f 20,485 | ✉ EMAIL | 🔄 SHARE | 🐦 TWEET |

Frederick M. Brown/Getty Images

Soap star Nancy Lee Grahn reiterated her disdain for the Trump family in a tweet posted Sunday, smearing White House Senior Advisor Ivanka Trump as a Nazi after she posted a picture of her family's new dog, Winter.

Trump tweeted a photo of her family's newest furry addition – or what she called "Arabella's birthday dream come true" – in a tweet to her 6.7 million Twitter followers Saturday. Grahn pounced and went on the attack.

"How darling. I see you skipped a rescue and went straight to an Aryan breeder. Does it sit and sieg heil yet?" Grahn said, making a clear Nazi reference.

Ivanka Trump ✔ @IvankaTrump · Jul 20, 2019

Meet Winter, Arabella's birthday dream come true and the newest member of the Kushner family! 🐾

View image on Twitter

Nancy Lee Grahn ✔
@NancyLeeGrahn

How darling. I see you skipped a rescue and went straight to an Aryan breeder. Does it sit and sieg heil yet?

♡ 4,283   8:53 AM - Jul 21, 2019

When the President's daughter, Ivanka Trump, got a cute little white dog as a pet, TV Soap star Nancy Lee Grahn noted the dog was white with blue eyes and suggested that Ivanka must herself be a racist "White Supremacist."

The homosexual crowd demonstrates.

Jussie Smollett, actor of TV's Empire series and his "F— Donald" T-shirt. Smollett was later arrested for staging a hate crime hoax.

BREITBART

NOLTE: JARED AND IVANKA COMPARED TO 'COCKROACHES' ON JAKE TAPPER'S CNN SHOW

 437 EMAIL SHARE TWEET

MANDEL NGAN/AFP/Getty Images

by JOHN NOLTE | 14 Mar 2019 |

▶   🎧 LISTEN TO STORY   3:09

CNN's Paul Begala compared Jared Kuchner and Ivanka Trump to "cockroaches," and Jake Tapper pretty much let him.

In what has become typical for Tapper's basement-rated *The Lead*, Tuesday's show wallowed in salacious gossip and personal attacks as Tapper hyped yet another anti-Trump book, this one alleging President Trump wanted to fire Jared and Ivanka, wanted to get them out of the White House.

Because reading comprehension is hard and hate makes you stupid, after hearing Trump wanted to fire his own daughter and son-in-law, Tapper still asked his guests: "What, what do you take from, from this book? Is it a sign that loyalty is, is preeminent with the Trumps?"

More hatred by proto-psychopaths, this time animosity toward President Trump's daughter, Ivanka, and husband, Jared.

More Accurate than The New York Times, Washington Post, CNN and MSNBC for Two Years and Counting!
Grand Opening of The Gateway Pundit Store – Click Here

GATEWAY PUNDIT · TRUTH · GET YOUR CONSERVATIVE SWAG
STORE GRAND OPENING · shop now!!

SHOCK VIDEO: UCLA Students Support Putting Trump Supporters Into Concentration Camps

f 15.2K Share   🐦 252 Tweet   ✉ Email

by Cristina Laila   February 25, 2019   475 Comments

Conservative activist Kaitlin Bennett went undercover at UCLA under the alias 'Jenna Talia' to ask the far-left students to sign a petition if they supported throwing Trump supporters into involuntary re-education camps.

Ms. Bennett donned a rainbow 'Equality' hat with a matching t-shirt and rainbow socks and a fake nose ring so she would fit right in with the SJWs on campus.

The leftists Ms. Bennett approached were excited about the idea of throwing conservatives into concentration camps.

Actress Julia Louis-Dreyfus wears a pink "pussy hat" at the Women's March against President Trump. Decades prior, women wore red "Illuminati" hats, signifying they were revolutionaries.

Democrat Ilhan Omar, the first female Somali-American Congressperson in U.S. House of Representatives, is a rabid Trump hater.

15 CELEBRITIES WHO BLAMED TRUMP, DEPLORABLES FOR HOAX ATTACK ON JUSSIE SMOLLETT

Rich Fury/Getty Images/Cindy Ord/Getty Images for SiriusXM

by JUSTIN CARUSO | 17 Feb 2019 | 19,981

Left-wing Hollywood wasted no time in politicizing and blaming President Donald Trump and his supporters for an alleged hate crime attack on *Empire* actor Jussie Smollett — an encounter that police now reportedly believe to have been staged.

CNN's Shimon Prokupecz reported Saturday, "Chicago Police believe Jussie Smollett paid two men to orchestrate the assault. The sources tell CNN that the two men are now cooperating fully with law enforcement."

> **Shimon Prokupecz** ✔
> @ShimonPro
>
> CNN: Chicago Police believe Jussie Smollett paid two men to orchestrate the assault.
> The sources tell CNN that the two men are now cooperating fully with law enforcement.
>
> ♡ 7,564   6:41 PM - Feb 16, 2019
>
> ○ 3,793 people are talking about this

'F**k your president!' Vape shop worker is FIRED after going on furious expletive-filled rant and refusing to serve a customer because he was wearing MAGA hat and Trump T-shirt

- Ian Furgeson, 36, filmed himself getting kicked out of a vape shop in Georgia
- He entered the shop on Friday to purchase some items for his wife but was asked to leave allegedly after the employee saw his MAGA hat and Trump shirt
- The employee at first respectfully asked him to leave but after Furgeson goads him he explodes and launches an expletive-filled rant
- He says: 'Get the f*** out of here. I f***ing can't stand y'all racist mother f***ers'
- Video of the furious rant has gone viral with over 7million views
- Furgeson says Xhale City's corporate office got in touch with him afterwards and told him the employee was fired
- Xhale City posted a status on Facebook saying they fired the clerk in light of the incident, then proceeded to delete all of their social media pages Friday evening

By MARLENE LENTHANG FOR DAILYMAIL.COM
PUBLISHED: 12:32 EST, 29 December 2018 | UPDATED: 15:10 EST, 29 December 2018

A Georgia vape shop worker launched an explosive rant against a Trump-supporting customer and refused to serve him in a shocking incident all caught on video.

Ian Furgeson, 36, walked into Xhale City in Tucker on Friday to buy some items but quickly bumped heads with the store employee who asked him to leave just minutes after he entered the shop.

Furgeson, sporting a MAGA hat and Trump shirt, then whipped out his phone and began to goad the store clerk.

'I have just been asked to leave the store. He greeted me, that was nice. I did find the item that I wanted and the next thing he said was he'd like me to leave,' Furgeson said.

Anger boiled up inside anti-Trump FBI agent Peter Strzok in 2017 during congressional hearings. His facial expression is undeniably hostile. Compare it to that of the actors below in a scene in a 1930s movie.

Chapter Six

The Stupid, Cruel, and Inhuman Psychopath

"We can and must write in a language which sows among the masses hate, revulsion and scorn toward those who disagree with us."
— Vladimir Lenin

Psychiatrists and other authorities estimate that about five percent (5%) of the general population are psychopaths. Since the United States population is approximately 330 million, this means that we find ourselves bombarded with about 16,500,000 psychopaths. Some, of course, are more dangerous than others. Their behavior is more lethal. Not all are evil serial killers, nor are the majority "Bernie Madoff" types—financial master thieves and scheming conmen. *But every psychopath is to be avoided.*

Thus, it is essential that we do our utmost to spot and identify the psychopath. To fail to do so is to truly invite the potential for tragedy into your life.

The majority of psychopaths hide in plain sight. They do not operate at the criminal level or else they do and just operate beneath the law enforcement red line. Some have high IQs, most do not, but every psychopath thinks they are superior to us, the normal people, whom they look upon as stupid and gullible, deserving only their contempt and their inhumanity.

We can identify the psychopath by his attitude, his lack of compassion, and his demonstrable desire for domination and control.

The Attitude of the Psychopath

First, his attitude. The psychopath is constantly on the lookout for his next target, his next "pigeon" as the small-time gangster might say. He is quite adept at identifying who is most likely to be manipulated and conned. The psychopathic politician is non-ideological, he or she has no reliable philosophical guidepost, but he is able to identify the fanatic, the "true believer" who does. He, therefore, centers in on this person. The psychopath uncannily becomes the perfect ideological host. He portrays himself as the ideal believer. "I believe exactly as you do," he constantly assures the chosen victim.

The political psychopath will continue with his fake persona until the deluded victim is in his grip, and until he is in total control.

This lack of authenticity on the part of the psychopath means that his personality and behavior is flexible and ever-changing. The psychopath makes an outstanding politician; in other words, a manipulating lying deceiver!

Thomas Sheridan, author of *Puzzling People: The Labyrinth of the Psychopath*, notes this camouflage strategy of psychopaths. He writes:

> "The psychopath literally has no idea how to be a human being and must pick up the skills as they go along. Let me repeat this once more so it sinks in. The psychopath literally does not know how to be a human being so it has to constantly practice in order to create a socially credible facsimile of one."

Please note that Sheridan aptly uses the pronoun "it" when referring to the psychopath. Like me and many others who have unraveled the pitiful truth about psychopaths, Sheridan sees these pseudo-persons as non-humans.

Sheridan goes on to explain that, "Until the victim starts to come to understand that what they were dealing with all along was not one of us. Then, at that moment, the victim and target begin to see the way out of the labyrinth."

Regrettably, until that point, the targeted victim, being a sincere, trusting individual, is easily bamboozled. He is relatively sure that the political psychopath, whom he views as a model and leader, will go through with his promises. His faith in the psychopath is shattered when the psychopath fails to produce as he committed. But if he confronts the psychopath, he is "gas-lighted." The psychopath uses a form of deceptive "Mr. Bojangles" language to trick the True Believer into accepting his betrayal.

This is why the U.S. Congress is designed as it is. First, the senator or representative votes one way, to approve or disapprove the project. But then comes a second vote, on which the senator or congressman may cast a totally different vote. "Oh, yes. I favor that project," says the lying representative. "That's why I voted 'yes' when it came up."

But that vote, as it turns out, was not the deciding vote. The representative may, the very next day even, vote "No" on funding the project. Thus, he can go both ways, pleasing all sides.

As Senator John Kerry once stated in regards to his vote on a particular bill, "I voted for it before I voted against it." He, of course, assumed that his gas light attempt carried both sides. Apparently, such a devious system is designed to deceive the masses, because most legislation goes back and forth, with a congressman voting this way, then that way.

However, the psychopath will never admit he or she has been inconsistent. He will, instead, makeup excuse after excuse, and lead you to believe that he is ever true to the chosen theme or ideology. The psychopath aligns himself with popular causes, appearing to be endowed with superior moral wisdom.

Robespierre, the leader of the French Revolution, was able to convince the people that "more blood" was necessary for the revolution to succeed. Likewise, Lenin and Stalin persuaded the people that it would, of course, take more lives, more blood for the Bourgeoisie to be vanquished and then, the people would be empowered and an eternal Democracy would be firmly established.

Until that "glorious day of victory" is achieved, those who oppose their vicious, inhuman criminal behavior, will be uprooted, smeared, charged with crimes they didn't commit, and painted as liars and abusers of the masses. Thus, a never-ending campaign is waged against the "enemies of the state."

Normal People Despised by the Psychopath

The normal people are the targets. Psychopaths detest normal people, because they, themselves, recognize they are different. They, the psychopaths, are to the normal person, *abnormal*. They embrace the bad and hate the good. They love lies and use them to conquer truthtellers. They view ugly as beautiful and sexual normality as grossly inadequate. They trumpet that their goal is to create a "Better World," but hide the fact that their "Better World" will be a pathetic mirror of their unnatural, perverted lifestyle.

For them, religion is vile and morality unacceptable. They seek to change religion, to persuade their populace that the established religion is unjust, that its "hero" (Jesus, for example) was just like the psychopath. Thus, they promote inversive thinking; the psychopathic leader inverts evil and good. The masses become confused; they adopt evil and eschew the good, and society becomes brutal and base. The wicked succeed, the good are debased and demoted.

Lack of Compassion

Psychopaths are demonstrably cruel and inhuman, but can we say they are stupid? True, some have high IQs. They are known to even deceive and trick their therapists, as many psychiatrists will attest. But their deceit and evil are eventually exposed. Though psychopaths are often calculating, there seems to be a gap in their thinking.

Husbands who are psychopaths can hide their sickness for a long period but eventually, it comes out. The psychopathic wife-beater is "nice" for days, weeks, or months but suddenly he snaps and again abuses his wife. This is because he has little respect for anyone but himself. After hitting or otherwise abusing his spouse, the psychopath, realizing he has gone too far, may backtrack and say he is sorry, that he won't do it again. He may add theatre to his performance, crying and wringing his hands, etc. But beware, he undoubtedly will repeat his bad behavior. It's just a matter of time.

Likewise, the psychopath who enjoys conning victims out of their money will, once caught and punished, strike again. And the political psychopath will repeatedly betray his constituents. It is his nature to lie, cheat, exaggerate, defraud and deceive.

Psychopaths are notoriously expert at lying to therapists. However, they do not seek out psychological help. They believe they need no help, that they are perfect just as they are. If they do see a therapist, it is usually court-directed or at the insistence of an abused spouse. The counseling does the psychopath little good. It often simply educates them on how to appear reasonable and sane in the future in spite of their psychopathic tendencies.

The psychopath enjoys cat and mouse games in therapy. He may attempt to persuade the therapist that he is the victim, that he is being mistreated. He may put on a false self, orchestrating a show, even pretending to be the suffering victim. The psychopath can be temporarily charming and fool the therapist into thinking that he is stable and reasonable.

This theatrical display has even convinced prison therapists to recommend early release for the psychopath whom they feel is "reformed" and "changed." Sometimes, the parole board will concur, and the psychopath is home free. Immediately, he reverts to his typical psychopathic behavior. Many real-life cases have been reported of psychopaths robbing banks or conning victims, etc., within days of release from prison as a "rehabilitated" convict.

Psychopaths Cannot Be Cured

The fact is, psychopaths *cannot* be cured. They are who they are. This leads to a worrisome concern for normal society. Their sentence is meted out according to the usual schedule of punishments. Then, they are unfortunately released, only to commit additional crimes.

Prison time is not a deterrence. Indeed, it often increases their desire to repeat and even to amplify their outrageous behavior. The attitude of the psychopath is basically, "So, this time I got caught. I'll be more careful next time. I'm smarter than the cops and there are so many dumb folks out there just waiting to be taken."

For the psychopath, the whole world is their oyster. They are different, they have no empathy for their victims, no reason not to continue their crime wave. So it's on to another target, and psychopaths are ever monitoring the landscape in a hungry search for victims. They are masters of deceit.

They Have an Advantage

Their cold-bloodedness and rejection of morality give the psychopath great advantages over their victims. Ted Bundy, who murdered 30 young women in his serial crime spree, was able to easily obtain the sympathy and pity of his targets. He would, for example, go to the beach, and spy a young girl alone sunning herself. Parking his car nearby and putting on a fake arm sling, he would hobble up and ask if the young woman would mind helping him by opening his car door. Naturally, most said, "Sure." Then, producing a gun or knife and overcoming his victim and pushing her into his car seat, Bundy would begin his horrible act.

Bundy was handsome and appeared genuine and so he was believable. In custody, he told the police, "I'm the most cold-blooded son of a bitch you'll ever meet. I just liked to kill."

Robert William "Willie" Pickton went on trial for murdering 26 women. He bragged to a cellmate that he had intended to kill 50 women. In his interrogations by Canadian law enforcement, Pickton was, like Ted Bundy, devoid of emotion. He showed no concern and no empathy for a single woman he had killed. Yet, evidence showed how brutal and demonic were his terrible crimes. Pickton degraded, tortured, and dismembered these poor women.

During his trial, those present in the courtroom were astonished over his lack of emotion when his crimes were described. Pickton appeared bored and distracted, and thoroughly detached from reality.

Gary Ridgway, the infamous Washington State Green River killer, sat placidly, casually and without emotion describing how he had cruelly killed 48 women. The victims were mere objects. Ridgway attempted at times during his interrogation to show remorse but eventually would revert back to his actual feelings — of nothingness and devoid of empathy. Challenged, he would sometimes express aggression and hostility toward his victim. It was, he said, all their fault. They goaded him, they belittled him, they were unworthy of living. He was able to snare them because of his superior intellect. This arrogance is typical of psychopaths.

They Are Different Than Are We

Experienced psychiatrists and others who have studied psychopaths report that the psychopath begins first to realize how different from normal people he or she is at about the age of 15. Perceptive parents and guardians sometimes recognize their inhuman instincts and odd attitudes much earlier, even as children.

It is said that upon entering a room full of people, the psychopath quickly begins to survey the scene. Uncannily, they are often able to spot and identify other psychopaths, even at a distance.

Christopher Berry-Dee, in the Foreword to Victoria Redstall's frightening portraits of serial killers in her book, *Serial Killers: Up Close and Very Personal*, says that whether male or female, psychopathic killers "represent monstrosities of the most terrifying variety."

> "They are human predators — in some cases, cannibals in a figurative and, often, literal sense — and are therefore uniquely subversive to society's carefully constructed behavioral tenets. They frighten us because they are part us, part monster, humanoid in form. They are without social conscience… They are morally dead… They personify the human capacity for evil."

Albert DeSalvo, known as the Boston Strangler, raped and murdered 13 women. His victims were between 19 and 85 years old. DeSalvo, like most psychopaths, began his brutality at age 15 by torturing defenseless animals. When caught, he had a long rap sheet, including beating his wife and many home burglaries. He was a big braggart and a known "peeping Tom." He murdered most victims in their homes where they lived alone. While in prison, DeSalvo was himself murdered by other inmates.

John Wayne Gacy was a businessman from the Chicago area. He was well-known for his volunteer work in the Democrat Party and once had his picture taken with First Lady Rosalyn Carter (lower left). Police searched his home on December 22, 1978, and found many bodies of murdered young men in the crawl space under his house. Gacy confessed to 33 murders and said some bodies he threw in the Des Plaines River.

Also shown is a picture of Gacy with his wife when married.

Psychopaths are multisexual. It doesn't matter if it is a male or female they have sex with. Gacy sexually abused and tortured young teenage boys.

Gacy entertained as "Pogo the Clown," visiting local hospitals. At his trial, he wise-cracked to the jury that he was guilty only of "running a cemetery without a license." In prison, he painted oil portraits of clowns and received up to $20,000 for each. At his execution on May 10, 1994, he was asked if he had any last words. Gacy remarked, "Kiss my ass."

Russian psychopath who dug up girls' bodies and turned them into dolls. Anatoly Moskvin, a 52-year-old historian from the Russian city of Nizhny Novgorod, was arrested and sentenced to compulsory psychiatric treatment after two dozen mummified bodies were discovered at his apartment.

POWER OF PROPHECY

Exclusive Intelligence Examiner Report

Texe Marrs

Poland Hunts Jewish Commandant Wanted For "Crimes Against Humanity"

Poland is demanding that Israel extradite for trial a Jewish man accused of brutal tortures and mass killings in a Soviet concentration camp.

Solomon Morel, 86, was commandant of a death camp at Swietochlowice, Poland after World War II. The camp's population included many innocent Polish men, women, and children of German descent whose homes, businesses and belongings had been seized by Jewish communist authorities. The victims were then herded into numerous concentration camps, one at Swietochlowice.

Morel was indicted in 1994 by a Polish court and ordered to face charges of "crimes against humanity." Among the crimes the Jewish commandant allegedly committed: murders by bashing the heads of babies against stone walls; bludgeoning inmates to death with stools and clubs; inflicting extreme pain by forcing objects up inmates' anus; forcing women and children to parade around nude in subfreezing temperatures; making inmates eat human feces; and starving people to death.

Upon his indictment, Solomon Morel, assisted by the Israeli government, fled to Tel Aviv, Israel where he has been hiding out. American television's 60 Minutes program tracked him down and located Morel in that city. His whereabouts are known to the Israeli authorities.

Up to 80,000 people are believed to have died as a result of torture, deprivation, and starvation in post-World War II concentration camps, all of which were headed by Jewish commandants.

According to a report in London's *The Telegraph,* newspaper (January 2, 2005) and in John Sack's investigative book, *An Eye for An Eye,* "Stalin deliberately picked Jews as camp commandants in the knowledge they would show little mercy to the inmates."

The Polish public prosecutor leading the Morel case, Eva Kok, insisted that the claims could not be "swept under the carpet." She added: "The Israelis are extremely efficient in pursuing people they have accused of such crimes—and they must accept that other nations want to do the same."

School Killers Hated Christians

Eric Harris and Dylan Klebold were mass murderers who, together, killed 13 people and wounded 24 others on April 20, 1999 at Columbine High School in Colorado. They were seniors at the school. Both were disliked by fellow students because of their thuggery and bullying. Police found on their home computers massive evidence of their hatred toward others and especially toward those who were Christians.

Eric Harris wrote online that he was superior to others who were weak and deserved to die. "I have a goal to destroy the whole world—and everybody in it," he wrote. "I hate them all." Klebold, his co-murderer, said he would make everyone pay for not including him in school activities and he made a list of those he intended to kill.

Both Harris and Klebold experimented joyously with their firearms, killing neighborhood cats and dogs and laughing at their suffering.

Harris bragged that he deserved an Oscar for duping his parents. The boys came from affluent middle class families and were well-treated by their parents. In the murder spree, they made Christians get down on their knees. Dylan asked one girl, "Do you love your Jesus?" "Yes," answered the frightened girl. "Then you're going to see him," said the hateful killer. With that said, he shot her between the eyes. The two, like other psychopaths, showed they had no conscience and no remorse. They ended up committing suicide.

Eric Harris and Dylan Klebold, posing for the camera—two sick and twisted psychopaths.

Dr. H. H. Holmes and His Chicago Hotel from Hell

Doctor H. H. Holmes was reputed to be one of the 19th century's most proficient mass killers, overall murdering numerous people, most of whom were young ladies. He began his gruesome life of crime by murdering the female owner of a drug store in Chicago where he worked as a young man. With money he obtained from the victims, he built a huge building downtown, with over 100 rooms and many secret passageways and spaces. When Chicago held the renowned World's Fair Columbian Exposition of 1893, Dr. Holmes began to rent rooms, preferring young ladies far from home.

As a boy, Holmes had pleasure in killing and dissecting pet dogs and cats. As an adult, he carried out this same evil work, except now on live young women. He murdered dozens of women, torturing them in sound-proof rooms. Some he put to sleep with chloroform and when they awoke, they found themselves encased between walls. Screaming and frightened, they slowly starved to death, unable to escape.

On November 17, 1894, he was arrested in Boston after an investigator found the bodies of three children Holmes had murdered.

Holmes is said to have killed up to 100 hapless victims. He was tried and hanged on May 7, 1896.

Chapter Seven

TranceFormation of Humanity

"Madness is something rare in individuals but in groups, parties, and peoples, it is the rule."

—Friedrich Nietzsche
Beyond Good and Evil

Have you ever, even for a moment, questioned your reality, your existence? Do you sometimes feel you are in a trance-like state? Have you ever considered that even as technology is galloping forward at a rapid pace, and change everywhere is epidemic, you and the rest of humanity are undergoing a dramatic transformation and that most people are locked in some sort of hypnotic trance, like the bewildered characters in Alice in Wonderland?

You are not alone. Today, as change is taking place in every sector of life, the thoughtful frequently stop and reflect, "Has the World Gone Mad?" or ask, "Are we living in a *Twilight Zone?*"

The startling answer is…Yes! And the world has gone mad by purpose, by craft, by design on the part of some very evil and cunning "change artists." Best stated, these evil and cunning people are societal *misfits*, afflicted but continually deceiving and misdirecting you and other normal people for their own wicked purposes. You, dear friend, have descended into the confusing, brutal labyrinth of the Psycho Zone. It is now the age of the coming of the psychopaths. And believe me, things will grow worse and worse.

Entering the Psycho Zone

It is not always possible to identify the exact moment in time when a nation has entered the Psycho Zone. But astute observers note that just prior to its beginning, what we might call a period of *Crazy Times* occurs. Suddenly, things begin to change, the nation seems to shift into high psychopathic gear. Sexual morals are changing, the concept of nationhood suffers deterioration, and education, movies and television express this new spirit of ridiculism. Music becomes angry and chaotic, laws are discarded, and God is scoffed at and considered passé.

During these *Crazy Times*, psychologists change their views about human nature. What was once considered psychologically an aberration is redeemed. Good becomes evil and vice versa. The Psychiatric Diagnostic Manual is readily reinterpreted as conservative views are jettisoned. They suddenly are considered obsolete and even as destructive.

Slowly, the general public accepts these *Crazy Times* as just good common sense, and those who oppose them are labeled dangerous and even as mentally disordered.

The Age of Psychopaths is an era when men and women quite *different* than you and me have, *en masse*, reached the upper levels of society. These are people who loathe traditional America and despise Christianity and its values. They know they do not fit into normal society, and that it is you and I versus them. They are determined to win, to dominate and they will not be stopped by society's mores and norms. Instead, they work to create a New America, unshackling themselves and punishing anyone who gets in their way.

So far, their efforts have given them great success, but they are never satisfied. Psychopaths are constantly moving the goalposts. Their internal world is a blizzard of double-mindedness, impulsivity, aggression, and recklessness. They show utter disregard for the safety and well-being of others. They are irresponsible in whatever *persona* they have molded. They view traditional society as stupid, irrelevant, and inferior and scheme to replace it with their own immoral, insane, cruel, senseless, and ever-changing creed of conduct. They feel no guilt for their lies and for the wreckage of humanity they leave in their wake. In fact, they rather enjoy the pain and chaos they cause others.

Theirs is a *Revolution*, which today they are winning. Triumphantly they maraud about the world, engaging in several key areas of revolutionary activity, causing confusion, panic and havoc wherever they engage. We look at seven such revolutionary areas in this book:

1. God

2. Nationalism vs. Globalism

3. Sex and Love

4. Education

5. Media

6. Technology

7. Culture

It is important to note that in constantly making erratic, confusing changes in society in these areas of life, psychopaths realize they are bringing about an over-all revolution. This revolution is now gathering steam, and America augurs to be a wholly different country very soon because of pathocratic domination. These psychopathocratic changes may well turn America into an unrecognizable *slave state*, devoid of freedom, with the citizenry barely able to survive the constant battering rams of psychopathocratic assault.

You will read in this book about the horrors that occurred in ancient Rome, in the U.S.S.R. during the communist era, in revolutionary France, and in Cambodia. These were all nations that fell victim to the terrors of psychopathy. Now, is it America's turn at the despotic wheel?

What is seen in America today is almost exactly what was witnessed in these historical psychopathic eras. We see the same *spell-binding* tactics employed by Robespierre, Stalin, and Hitler. Most importantly, each era shows definite signs of the mass public falling prey to what we can call *Consensus Trance*.

Consensus Trance is a hypnotic spell that afflicts the masses, making them prone to believing the lies and deceit practiced by the psychopathic leaders in charge. Few people can avoid this hypnotic spell. The masses are persuaded that they alone are morally and intellectually superior and that the remainder must be closely monitored and punished for their failure to adopt the new psychopathic norms.

Victims of Consensus Trance

The most devious of the psychopaths who aggressively plot to take over a nation are *spell-binders*. Their charm, charisma and gifts of lying and deceit enable them to attract large audiences. Media adoration propels their popularity and assist their building of *Consensus Trance*. This consensus is based on their manipulative ability to make outrageous promises to voters and supporters. An honest opponent cannot possibly keep up with the largess promised by the psychopath.

The psychopath appeals to the voters' base instincts. Whatever the crime and sin or career and life advancement the voter wants to engage in is approved by the psychopath leader—abortion, infanticide, illegal drugs, crooked welfare payments, free sex, free college tuition, free medical, better job—*"You name it and I'll get it for you,"* he or she boldly claims. *"Forget the budget, forget the Constitution, forget the laws. It's reward time baby!"*

As Lenin promised, "all power to the people."

Who will pay for all this? Why the rich, of course. We'll just raise taxes on the super-rich, says the psychopath.

The psychopath further insinuates that he will not judge the voter for his indiscretions: "I'm a Progressive," he shouts out. "Do as you will shall be the whole of the law."

"There is no God, no Judge up in the sky," says the psychopath. "So don't listen to the conservative and traditional hypocrite."

Who can beat this grand promise? The *Crazy Times* will continue on, unabated, the voter decides, as his reason is dispelled and he joins in the *Consensus Trance*. Spell-binding, the molding of minds by the elite, works in the psychopathocratic nation.

Chapter Eight

Now is the Time of Monsters: 13 Factors that Work to Create a Psychopathic Nation

"The old world is dying, and the new world struggles to be born; now is the time of monsters."

— Antonio Gramsci

From our study of history, we can gauge facts necessary for the rise of psychopaths in a nation. In every nation and every era we find individuals with psychopathic tendencies and behavior. Some historians claim that if there were no psychopaths there would be no wars and no conflict between nations. They believe that, absent psychopathic individuals, mankind would enjoy peace and justice, harmony and love. They may not be far from the truth.

Psychopaths exact a terrible toll on society and are responsible for a large part of the murders, scams, and other societal miseries. It is therefore of utmost importance that we are able to understand the reasons that a nation opens itself up to the ravages caused by psychopathic criminals.

Only if these conditions exist and are exaggerated in a nation do psychopaths gain public trust. Only then is it possible for the psychopath to be promoted and reign. If, however, the nation's moral fiber is sufficient, these factors do not present themselves and psychopaths fail in their perverted desire to dominate and control.

There are thirteen factors, or conditions, in a nation that contribute to the growth of psychopaths and the psychopaths' rise to power. We will cover each for it is these thirteen factors that have created in America the *Crazy Times* that indicate the emerging first stage of a Psychopathic Nation. It is this strange and frightening time of turbulence and chaos in which we are now immersed.

Thirteen Conditions of Crazy Times in America Leading to a Psychopathic Takeover

1. *Devaluation of Youth:* Young people are devalued by society, beginning with the embrace of abortion. Few real jobs are available and parents and grandparents must provide financial support. Unprepared for the maturing required by marriage, and universally uneducated, many youths live at home.

They marry later or not at all. Their minds are confused by a hodge-podge of fake news piped into their minds by the internet. Their minds are also clouded by computer games, and by TV and movies on topics such as zombies, dystopia, and far-out wars and conflict. Political candidates cater to their immature, juvenile minds.

The Psychopathic Devil and the Abortion Horror

Dr. Kermit Gosnell was an abortion doctor who worked out of this clinic in Philadelphia. In 2011, the Doctor, whom some called the "Devil," murdered untold numbers of infants. Many abortions by Gosnell were late term and some babies he killed after they were born. He would bring the baby out of the womb and if it was still alive, he would use scissors to cut the infant's spine. He performed hundreds of illegal abortions and in one case he and his assistant grabbed a woman bodily and forced her on his operating table after the woman had changed her mind. Investigators said his offices were filthy, he rarely washed his operating tools, and feces and urine were everywhere. In the basement, investigators found dead body parts, and the heads of aborted babies stuffed into glass jars. Gosnell received $10,000 to $15,000 per operation. He sometimes failed to use an anesthetic and women reported severe pain. One died. Gosnell laughed and bragged that one baby that came out was "so big he was ready to walk around my office." He killed that baby. Gosnell was tried and is in a Pennsylvania prison for life without the possibility of parole. The media, favorable to abortion, refused to report the horrors done at the clinic.

2. *Socialism Favored Over Capitalism:* Polls show that a majority of youth, ignorant of history but aware of economic inequities in society, favor socialistic economics over capitalism. They want free college, free medical care, free psychological counseling, free rent, etc. They believe socialism will be paid for by the rich. However, as Lenin observed, "Socialism leads to Communism." Yet, today's youth know little about the ravages and horrors of Communism.

3. *Class Warfare:* Politicians promote rivalry and discord between the races and ethnic groups and between women (a favored class) and men. There is constant talk of toxic masculinity, women warriors, and racism. Ages are also examined and "old white men" are hated. The elite despise the Deplorables, and minorities and foreigners are favored by legislatures over the common citizenry.

4. *De-Christianization:* Society is de-Christianized. A "New Morality" is promoted, with perverted sex at its center and sin exalted. Liberal churches that employ a new language of inclusion and present a "new Jesus" of love and peace take hold. The concept of judgment is neglected. Denominationalism is dying out as churches change their names to reflect the new religious universalism. Christians are pushed to answer whether for some 2,000 years they have been carriers of prejudice and hostility to homosexuality and transgenderism. Also, they are forced by public pressure to abandon their exclusivity and to embrace other religions and beliefs such as Islam, Hinduism, and Atheism. Even blatant satanism and witchcraft are celebrated by many.

5. *Sexual Debauchery:* Movie stars openly declare they are sluts and are "nasty women" to the cheers of roaring crowds. Homosexuals and lesbians demand equal—and more than equal—recognition. Drag queens flaunt their extreme appearance and are invited into classrooms of elementary schools and to libraries to indoctrinate unknowing, innocent children. TV shows and movies celebrate sexual perversion and promote abortion and sexual kinkiness. Transgender bathrooms come into vogue and rape is often considered by judges to be a physical necessity rather than a heinous crime. The age of consent is lowered; pornography is widely available even to the young, and prostitution is deemed acceptable.

6. *Vulgar, Coarse Language:* Dirty words ("F...Y...") are accepted and become a staple. Teachers, CEOs, even the President of the United States are targets of slanderous, nasty language. Filthy language is a prominent feature on TV and in movies. Free speech is seen by many as offensive and violent, while vulgarity is widespread.

7. *Music:* Sociologists have noted that music has become degraded and is laden with violence, anger, and sexual perversions.

8. *Collapse of Education:* Educational processes as judged by standardized exams are failing. From kindergarten to higher education (university level) this is

true. Teachers and professors lower expectations and reward students according to social class. Bizarre topics precious to the goals of liberals and progressives are taught. Admissions standards and grading at universities are lowered so that minorities and foreign students can be admitted. Society begins to look askance and to demean education. Textbooks are diminished. Faculties are made up predominantly of liberal individuals hostile to tradition.

| Larry Page Alphabet/Google | Mark Zuckerberg Facebook | Tim Cook Apple | Jack Dorsey Twitter | Jeff Bezos Amazon |

Make Way For the Social Media Giants

They are called the Masters of the Universe. They are the CEOs of the world's most powerful social media corporations. Billionaires, all are left wing progressives. They are "planetarians," dismiss America and are hostile to everything America stands for, except its money. Together, they are stamping out conservative websites and abolishing Christian views. They consider themselves the "Democratic elite" and despise the Republicans and their Deplorables. Are the Masters of the Universe psychopaths? Certainly they foster the emergence of America as a *Psychopath Nation.*

9. *History of America Diminished:* America is taught by education to be a wicked, militant nation guilty of slavery, genocide, racial bigotry, sexual horrors, and toxic masculinity. Our founding fathers, Washington, Jefferson, Adams, *et al*, are said to have been evil plantation slave owners and tyrants. Textbooks and painted murals are revised, and statues of great men—now deemed "Old White Men"—are being removed and destroyed. Everywhere their names are being removed, and airports, streets, schools, cities and towns are being renamed with liberals and progressive women and men being honored in their place. World War I and II are considered eras of American assault and crude racism. Native indigenous peoples are celebrated and white people are seen as racist exploiters.

10. *Political Corruption:* Political corruption is rampant with both Republicans and Democrats taking bribes and kickbacks from foreign and domestic lobbyists. The average citizen is sneered at, foreigners and minorities are favored by tax/spend programs. Illegal immigration is promoted by the elite class to the detriment of the lower and working economic classes.

11. *Grandiose Schemes Abound:* Both political parties promote expansive and outrageous programs. Open borders are advocated. Climate change is taught to the masses with false verification by science. The gullible believe the world will soon end. A "Green New Deal" is touted. Reparations for blacks and a

Universal Base Pay scheme is promoted. Almost everything is to be free.

12. *Wars/Conflicts:* America is expected to be the Global Cop and its military is active in over 130 nations across the globe. But military personnel are looked down on by the elite who consider them inferior beings.

13. *Relative Deprivation:* This is the situation that takes the nation into a tipping point when added to other factors. It is the "revolution of rising expectations" when, after a long period of prosperity, the nation experiences an unexpected financial crisis. The French Revolution occurred in 1789 following a period of rising prosperity. Expectations were not met and a rebellion ensued. Alexis de Tocqueville wrote of this in his book, *Regime and Revolution* (1856). Philosopher Eric Hoffer observed that, oddly, people revolt only when things have gotten better. Disappointment over a sudden setback to their financial circumstances results in anger and rebellion.

In 1962, American sociologist James C. Davis published an article on what he called the J-curve hypothesis. He postulated that social and political unrest occurred when a nation had a sharp decline in the economy after a prolonged period of economic growth and development. Since the 2008 Great Recession, America has enjoyed economic expansion, first in the eight years of Barack Obama, then accelerating in the Donald Trump era. If, after this economic good fortune, another recession and an unexpected setback were to occur, combined with all other *Crazy Times* events, would dissatisfied workers rebel? Could cunning psychopaths, waiting in the shadows, see this rebellion as their opportunity to take over America and exercise their evil power?

The Monsters Have Arrived

A psychopathic age is already dawning in America as we descend into *Crazy Times*. Some may disagree that these thirteen factors, or conditions, are negative. They may argue that these extreme things are instead symptomatic of progress. or even as signs of liberation. They are wrong. This new era is different—*radically different.*

This is an age of the fall of church doctrine and practice, the rise of homosexuality and transgenderism, a mania over climate change, and much more. These are, indeed, *Crazy Times*, no matter how popular or contagious they may be, and *Crazy Times* is a dangerous period when psychopathic behavior rises and proliferates. Now is, indeed, the time of monsters.

Chapter Nine

Crazy Times: Early Reign of the Psychopaths

"You could put half of Trump's supporters into what I call the basket of deplorables. Right? The racist, sexist, homophobic, xenophobic, Islamphobic, you name it… I am all that stands between you and the Apocalypse."

> —Hillary Clinton
> LGBT For Hillary Gala
> (Sept. 10, 2016)

In America today at the present time, two main groups of citizens have evolved. What are these two groups? Some say it is the Democratic and Republican Parties. It is a fact that, generally, our nation is split along party lines, with *progressives* (Liberals) being the Democratic Party and *traditionalists* (Conservatives) tending to be the adherents of the Republican Party.

In the 2016 presidential election, in a noted speech, Democratic candidate Hillary Clinton referred to many supporters of Republican Donald Trump as a "Basket of Deplorables." They are, she scolded, "racist, sexist, homophobic, xenophobic, Islamophobic—you name it."

"And he has lifted them up," she said of Donald Trump. "Now some of these folks," Hillary continued, "are irredeemable."

Rejecting Hillary's remarks, Trump supporters surprisingly turned the tables by embracing them. They began to laughingly refer to themselves as both a "Basket of Deplorables" and as the "Irredeemables," or simply as the "Deplorables."

The *Deplorables* saw themselves as far different than Hillary's legions of *Progressives.* Their enthusiastic support for Donald Trump in the 2016 election resulted in one of the greatest political upsets in U.S. history. The *Deplorables* won for Trump the support of what we might call "Middle America," while Hillary's voters easily won the nation's liberal bastions, California and the west coast, Illinois and the east, New Jersey, New York, etc.

Progressives Went Crazy in Opposition

Following the election, Progressives everywhere went crazy in protest. All their wild instincts flowed outward and for some years all of America has been feasted to the *Crazy Times* of the Progressives. The Progressives, generally stated, are angry haters, foul-mouthed, ignorant, politically correct, unAmerican, riotous, troublemakers. Led by an incredible number of actual psychopaths, the Progressives are leading the nation in the *Crazy Times* period. Unwittingly perhaps, their rebellion and angry hatred of both America and the Deplorables has opened the door to the psychopath who cherishes the opportunity to abandon all reason and decimate all semblances of law and order.

The psychopath loves an angry mob of belligerent, but foolish people. He is possessed and has absolutely no conscience. He can easily bring down people who are superior to him in intellect because of his promises to "slay the opposition" and his constant lies and bullying. The vulnerable masses are prone to overlook his mistakes and miscalculations.

"Yes, the psychopath may be brutal and cold. Yes, he may bend the rules. But he is courageous in standing up for us," the Progressive says. *"And he wants what we want,"* they conclude.

And what is that? The psychopath demands the duly elected President and all his train of supporters be dethroned. He further insists that the Progressives, his growing band of proto-psychopaths (semi-psychopaths), be permitted to run amok in society. That is the beauty and appeal of the psychopath—no discipline, just anarchy, no punishment, just satisfaction and winning. His exuberant and excited throng of true believers rages on. The *Crazy Times* continues unabated.

The Crazy Times Have Exploded

The signs that America has already fallen victim to the psychopaths are all around us. It is unmistakable. Change is the catchword of psychopathy and everything is quickly changing. This is only partly due to technological advancements. For the most part, change—dramatic change—is now occurring as a result of psychopathic initiatives. Is this astonishing situation difficult for readers to accept? Then consider the *Crazy Times* that have descended upon us.

Preston James, a social psychologist, in his perceptive article, *"The Secret Law of Opposites,"* remarks, "The hardest thing about all this is just how strange and unexpected it is, that such an imaginably small group of criminally insane psychopaths could take over the whole world."

James is convinced these people, this "gang" of psychopaths are truly evil, but with a nice face and very effective powers for deceiving the naïve public, which tends to view them as benevolent parent figures.

"These select few," he says, "who sit at the top of this World Hierarchy of Evil control all the key institutions, large corporations and the existing establishment... If any public person publicly crosses them and goes outside allowed parameters, they will be sanctioned and often blacklisted to varying degrees from participating in the system in any meaningful way."

The principle of the psychopathic leaders who now rule covertly over us, James reports, is based on the idea that, "In order to establish a whole new globalist New World Order system, the existing natural order must be destroyed."

The idea that a conspiracy exists among the elite for a New World Order has long been laughed at and scorned by the mass media. But now we see that, just as President Donald Trump has exposed, the mass media are nothing more than stooges, dupes for the elite. They are paid shills who lie and deceive in order to please their Masters.

The truth of a widespread conspiracy led by money and psychopaths is apparent, but it may be far too late to stop the psychopathic contagion from spreading. America and the world seem to be in the firm grip of the beast, regardless of the Deplorables rebellion inspired by Donald Trump.

The Infestation is Nearing Completion

"I submit," writes Jack Mullen in a recent article (*Zerohedge.com*), "that the United States government is under the control of psychopaths, and the infestation is nearing completion; the point at which nothing can stop the coming violence."

Mullen authoritatively quotes Andrew Lobaczewski, psychiatrist and author of *Political Ponerology*, to buttress his contention. Lobaczewski, outlining the psychopathic madness that occurred during the Communist era in the Soviet Union and Eastern Europe, writes:

"In a pathocracy, all leadership positions…must be filled by individuals with corresponding psychological deviations…

"Under such conditions no area of social life can develop normally, whether in economic, culture, science, technology, administratively, etc.

"Pathocracy progressively paralyzes everything."

Do Lobaczewski's pungent writings not explain why almost everything in modern America seems odd and somehow eerily alien and different to normal, that is, traditional, society? The psychopaths are in charge and are pulling the train, moving us ever onward to a crunching conclusion as the natural order is overturned.

Is this not why the establishment has turned on Donald Trump with venomous anger? The psychopaths and their proteges see Trump as a regressive nationalist (*America First*) and an opponent of their new and rapidly rising *globalist order*. His election was a complete surprise to this ardent corps of anarchic plotters. *It cannot be tolerated.* Trump and his entire band of irredeemables and deplorables must be dealt with in a harsh and debilitating fashion.

Contempt For America by the Crazed Progressives

It was Robespierre, executioner during the French Revolution, who declared, "Pity is Treason." As for Trump, the many proto-psychopaths and their underlings, repel us with their sick and disgraceful threats (*"f__ you;" Let's impeach the MF___," "Lop off their heads,"* etc.).

These words, also of Robespierre, should be heeded:

"It is with regret that I pronounce the fatal truth: Louis ought to perish rather than a hundred thousand virtuous citizens; Louis must die that the country may live."

Is this an idle warning? Are there among the large and growing psychopathic element those who would do our President harm? Of course, there are. And remember, the Secret Service, the CIA, the FBI, and other intel agencies are implicated in the 1963 assassination of President John F. Kennedy. Today, their deterioration and lack of morality are even more pronounced. The recent coup attempt by FBI Director James Comey, his Deputy Andy McCabe, Agent Peter Strzok, the Justice Department's Rod Rosenstein, and others against the presidency of Donald Trump is indicative of their bias against Trump's *America First* policy and their unnatural contempt for the American Constitution and the "smelly Walmart people" (Strzok's description of Hillary's infamous, "Deplorables").

Trump has signaled his intention to thwart the globalists' (the psychopaths) plans. The globalists are going insane over this.

Trump, for example, discounts the Progressive theory of "climate change." Yet liberal Congresswoman Alexandria Ocasio-Cortez and other ignorant environmental whackos claim the world will end in twelve years or less. Would this alone not give the psychopaths and their angry ilk occasion to consider removing the President from office?

Better to be rid of him, that he "perish," than "a hundred thousand virtuous citizens" be extinguished by the catastrophe caused by climate change.

The Media are "In the Tank" for the Psychopathic Order

Polls show that 92% of the media voted Democratic for Hillary Clinton in the 2016 election. Other surveys indicate that the mass media trash President Trump in 90% of their news features covering the White House. This is yet another example of the psychopaths taking over the establishment.

Even in 2019, when immigration problems boiled over and threatened to capsize America, the mass media refused to affirm the President's warning on the Immigration crucible. "There is no crisis," repeated the media's mouthpieces over and over. The media trashed Trump's warnings even as *Breitbart*, a newsgroup separate from the establishment's news lackeys, ran a headline; "*Gallup: Five Million Latin Americans Coming to U.S. in next 12 months.*"

Nothing more than a "fabrication," echoed the news corps at *CNN, MSNBC, CBS, NBC, The Washington Post*, etc.

The Pathocracy's influence in the media establishment is remarkable. This substantial influence has become almost universal today, but it seems to have really taken firm hold since the advent of television. Professor Daniel Boorstin, Librarian of Congress (1975 to 1987) once stated, "Americans live in a world of pseudo-facts, which is created for them by their own media." This is, in fact, the primary reason that the citizenry today is in mental subjection to Consensus Trance.

Juri Lina, author of *Architects of Deception*, writes, "In our world…if something here happened but is not reported by the mass media, then it has simply not occurred. But if something has not even taken place and yet is reported in the media, then it has nonetheless happened."

Lina quotes Karl Marx as saying, "If you can cut people off from their history, they can be easily persuaded."

The Media Despise Free Speech

Psychopaths, being liars and manipulators and creators of false history, highly value the media's press censorship and fake news. Al Neuharth, the late publisher of *USA Today*, reported that in 1978, he and other editors had visited the headquarters of *Pravda*, the newspaper of the Communist Party and of the Soviet Government. They were startled to see these words chiseled into the big newsroom wall:

"Why should freedom of speech and freedom of the press be allowed? Why should a government which is doing what it believes right, allow itself to be criticized? It would not allow opposition by lethal weapons, and ideas are more fatal than guns."
—Vladimir Lenin, 1920

Lenin had voiced exactly the strong opinion of a psychopath, of which he was one. The opposition cannot be allowed the power of freedom of speech and of the press, nor any power outside that allowed by the psychopathic elite. As Lobaczewski writes in *Political Ponerology*: "To mitigate the threat to their power, the pathocrats must employ any and all methods of terror and exterminatory policies against individuals known for their patriotic feelings…"

The Educational Establishment Has Fallen Victim to Psychopathy

The Pathocracy's disastrous effects are especially found in the educational establishment from elementary schools to institutions of higher learning. Students everywhere are learning how "evil" is American nationalism, our nation's founding fathers, and the Constitution. And they are taught about the obsolete belief system of the discredited "Deplorables." In one survey on university campuses, a majority of students actually supported putting Trump supporters into concentration camps!

The Social Media Also Hate Traditional America

The anti-American, pro-pathocracy sentiment of the Social Media corporations— Facebook, Google, Twitter, Wikipedia, *et al*, is especially appalling—and frightening. The odd behavior of these fabulously rich haters of traditional values and conservatism is evident. Consider this excerpt of an interview of Twitter CEO Jack Dorsey by *Rolling Stone* magazine, in which Dorsey discusses his dining experience with Facebook mogul, Mark Zuckerberg:

"What was your most memorable encounter with Zuckerberg?

"Well there was a year when he was only eating what he was killing. Made goat for me for dinner. He killed the goat.

"In front of you?

"No. He killed it before. I guess he kills it. He kills it with a laser gun and then the knife. Then they send it to the butcher.

"A…laser gun?

"I don't know. A stun gun. They stun it, and then he knifed it. Then they send it to a butcher. Evidently in Palo Alto there's a rule or regulation that you have six livestock on any lot of land, so he had six goats at the time. I go, 'We're eating the goat you killed?' He said 'yeah.' I said, 'Have you eaten goat before?' He's like, 'Yeah, I love it.' I'm like, 'What else are we having?' 'Salad.'

"I said, 'Where is the goat?' 'It's in the oven.' Then we waited for about 30 minutes. He's like, 'I think it is done now.' We go in the dining room. He puts the goat down. It was cold. That was memorable. I don't know if it went back in the oven. I just ate my salad."

Facebook's goat-eater, Mark Zuckerberg, Twitter's Jack Dorsey, and other Social Media moguls hold tremendous power in America today and, indeed, throughout the world. Their online vehicles reach *billions* of readers. But all are hostile to the traditionalist viewpoints and they are continually removing real news and traditional websites from their platforms. In so doing, they are playing into the psychopaths' hands and are showing us that they buy into Vladimir Lenin's warped, anti-free speech ideology.

Confirmed Globalists, But Are They Human?

These Social Media moguls are confirmed *globalists*. They care little for the American Republic and its constitutional principles. As such, one has to ask, are these men (and women in some cases) psychopaths? A psychopath, as I have detailed, is not a human being, though he displays certain physical characteristics of humans.

Brandon Smith, in *Alt-Market.com* (republished in *Zero Hedge*, May 16, 2018) wrote the following:

"After studying the behavior of globalists and their organizations for quite some time, I have noticed that their psychological patterns tend to match with a narrow band of people that are best described as 'criminally insane.' More accurately, globalists behave like high-functioning sociopaths and psychopaths."

Smith goes on to illustrate that the traits of globalists and those of psychopaths dovetail significantly. He thus makes this eye-opening conclusion. *"Global elitists are not human… They are something opposite, and if you do not understand this core truth, they can be bewildering and terrifying."*

Politics   Entertainment   Media   Economy   World ⌄   Video   Tech   Sports

BREITBART

TRENDING: MASTERS OF THE UNIVERSE   ILHAN OMAR   MUELLER FAIL   FED DEATH PENALTY   EPSTEIN DRAMA

GALLUP: FIVE MILLION LATIN AMERICANS COMING TO U.S. IN NEXT 12 MONTHS

f   29,990   ✉ EMAIL   🔴 SHARE   🐦 TWEET

Joe Raedle/Getty Images

by PENNY STARR | 9 Feb 2019 | 💬 12.824

▶   🎧 LISTEN TO STORY   2:54

Five million Latin Americans plan to migrate to the United States in the next 12 months, and an estimated 42 million more say they want to enter the country.

Those statistics were in a report from Jim Clifton, the chairman and CEO at Gallup:

> Forty-two million seekers of citizenship or asylum are watching to determine exactly when and how is the best time to make the move. This suggests that open borders could potentially attract 42 million Latin Americans. A full 5 million who are planning to move in the next 12 months say they are moving to the U.S.

Chapter Ten

Crazy Times Gallery

The psychopaths in society inspire their spellbound throng of true believers to act out their combined expressions of insanity. Now, in this fertile, fast-growing *Age of the Psychopaths*, they can let loose their once bottled up anger and emotions. They can demonstrate their extreme sexuality, badger and persecute the hated "others," and show how much they despise society's moral values and devalue God and country.

Here are just a few recent pictures and news clippings from the mass media illustrating the *Crazy Times* plague of the psychopaths and their legions of supporters.

Crazytimes:

Gays and transgenders who have been told by psychologists that their attire and behavior are socially acceptable march to protest "normal" people.

PEW: U.S. CHRISTIAN POPULATION IN FREEFALL, 12% DROP IN TEN YEARS

| f 14,919 | ✉ EMAIL | ☻ SHARE | 🐦 TWEET |

Stefan Kunze/Unsplash

by THOMAS D. WILLIAMS, PH.D. | 18 Oct 2019 | **9382**

▶ 🎧 LISTEN TO STORY 2:58

Christianity in the United States is declining at an unprecedented rate, a new study by the Pew Research Council revealed Thursday, and the percentage of Christians in the country has hit an all-time low.

In just ten years the percentage of U.S. adults that identify as Christians dropped by a remarkable 12 percent, Pew found, from to 77 percent to just 65 percent, the lowest point in the nation's 243-year history.

Protestantism and Catholicism have both suffered significant losses, with the number of Protestants dropping from 51 percent in 2009 to just 43 percent today, while the number of Catholics has fallen from nearly a quarter of the population (23 percent) to just one-in-five (20 percent) since 2009.

During the same period, the number of religious "nones" — those who self-identify as atheist, agnostic, or "nothing in particular" — has shot up by a stunning 17 percent and this group now makes up more than a quarter of the population (26 percent).

The number of atheists in the country has doubled since 2009, from just 2 percent of the population to the current 4 percent. Agnostics now make up 5 percent of the adult population, up from just 3 percent in 2009, while those who describe their religion as "nothing in particular" has leapt from 12 percent to 17 percent in this ten-year period.

In absolute terms, the number of religiously unaffiliated adults in the U.S. has grown by almost 30 million since 2009.

The increase of the religiously unaffiliated has been most acute among young adults, resulting in a markedly less religious generation. Fewer than half of Millennials (49

BREITBART

GREENPEACE FOUNDER: GLOBAL WARMING HOAX PUSHED BY CORRUPT SCIENTISTS 'HOOKED ON GOVERNMENT GRANTS'

NASA/AFP/Chris LARSEN

by ROBERT KRAYCHIK   7 Mar 2019

Greenpeace co-founder and former president of Greenpeace Canada Patrick Moore described the cynical and corrupt machinations fueling the narrative of anthropocentric global warming and "climate change" in a Wednesday interview on SiriusXM's *Breitbart News Tonight* with hosts Rebecca Mansour and Joel Pollak.

Moore explained how fear and guilt are leveraged by proponents of climate change:

> Fear has been used all through history to gain control of people's minds and wallets and all else, and the climate catastrophe is strictly a fear campaign — well, fear and guilt — you're afraid you're killing your children because you're driving them in your SUV and emitting carbon dioxide into the atmosphere and you feel guilty for doing that. There's no stronger motivation than those two.

BREITBART

CALIFORNIA VETERANS HOME THREATENS TO EJECT 84-YEAR-OLD WIDOW FOR BIBLE STUDY GROUP

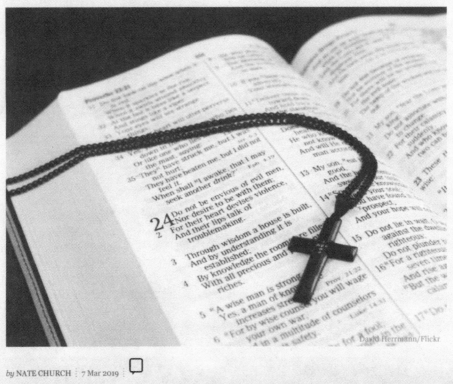

for *David Herrmann/Flickr*

by NATE CHURCH ┊ 7 Mar 2019 ┊

The Veterans Home of California in Yountville has threatened "involuntary discharge" if Artis Breau does not step down as a volunteer Bible study leader.

Breau came to the home with her husband nearly a decade ago and has spent much of that time volunteering with the chaplaincy program — and leading Bible studies — in the Holderman Building. Breau is being asked to relinquish her volunteer position over a discussion with a resident regarding Heaven and Hell that was deemed "elder abuse, emotional abuse, and otherwise illegal," after it allegedly caused him to lose sleep.

According to a statement by Lindsey Sin, deputy secretary at the California Department of Veterans Affairs:

> The safety, security, and wellbeing of all of our residents is our top priority. We are very proud of the religious services provided to all of our residents through our chaplaincy services. This investigation concerns the private conduct of an individual. Beyond that, we are unable to comment on an ongoing investigation.

BREITBART

ASSYRIAN WARNS AMERICANS TO VISIT ILHAN OMAR'S DISTRICT: YOU WON'T THINK IT'S AMERICA

2,428

by MICHELLE MOONS | 6 Mar 2019 | Washington, DC | 901

▶   🎧 LISTEN TO STORY   2:40

WASHINGTON, D.C. — Middle Eastern Women's Coalition (MEWC) director Nahren Anweya on Wednesday warned Americans who visit Minnesota's 5th district, Rep. Ilhan Omar's district, the 2016 "terrorist recruitment capital of the country."

"You won't even think you're in America," she said of the district that elected Ilhan Omar.

MEWC Director of Speical Projects Anweya was speaking at an MEWC press conference calling for Rep. Omar to resign. She said she has cousins and family members "called whores for showing" part of the back of the arm in Iraq, "a country where one day they were wearing mini skirts."

"It is truly because of people like [Rep.] Ilhan [Omar], when the government is infiltrated and it starts this way because it happened in Iraq and it happened against us," she went on. "Iraq used to be a country where Jews lived freely, where Assyrian Christians lived freely, where even Armenians were there, and even moderate Muslims lived until sharia law took place and everyone was affected."

"Americans truly need to understand that this will affect you one day if you don't make a change right now," she said of sharia, adding she knows the early signs of genocide.

BREITBART

GLORIA STEINEM COMPARES PRO-LIFE MOVEMENT TO NAZISM: HITLER 'CAMPAIGNED AGAINST ABORTION'

7,068

Alen K...Kea/... Images for MAKE...

by BEN KEW | 27 Feb 2019 | 3,197

▶ ︵ LISTEN TO STORY 2:07

Left-wing feminist activist Gloria Steinem compared supporters of the pro-life movement in America to Nazi Germans on the grounds that Adolf Hitler was against abortion for certain ethnic groups.

Appearing on NBC's *Today* show on Tuesday to promote the third edition of her book *Outrageous Acts and Everyday Rebellions*, Steinem referred to Hitler's position on abortion in the context of recent debates over what constitutes life.

"The new generation of reader is instructing me by saying that these essays are still relevant," she explained. "On a more serious note, to put it mildly, is why Hitler was actually elected, and he was elected and he campaigned against abortion. I mean, that was — he padlocked the family planning clinics. Okay, so that is still relevant in the terms of the right wing."

Daily Caller - https://dailycaller.com

Liberals Have Lost Their Collective Mind

etty Images/Mario Tama and Bill Pugliano

DEREK HUNTER
CONTRIBUTOR

February 26, 2019
8:46 AM ET

On the show today, we count the way in which the political left has lost their collective minds. Sen. Bernie Sanders wants control over everything, Rep. Alexandria Ocasio-Cortez wants to spend almost $100 trillion, and former Vice President Joe Biden demands no brown M&Ms in his dressing room. Also, activists in Virginia watched NYC chase away Amazon and 25,000 jobs and are trying to replicate that, Senate Democrats vote to keep infanticide, and a gay rights activist is charged with burning down his own house in a fake hate crime. We cover it all on today's show.

In a CNN town hall, Bernie Sanders accidentally admitted he's looking to strip health insurance from the millions of Americans who are happy with their private plans in the name of the collective good. In exchange, Sanders is promising the sun, the moon, and the stars, and all for "free!" We've heard this song before and are still waiting for our $2,500 in average savings per family from Obamacare. We have the audio and the truth.

Alexandria Ocasio-Cortez didn't attach a price tag to her "Green New Deal," possibly because she can't count. But it's more likely that it's because she doesn't want people to know. Well, a former director of the Congressional Budget Office

High School Transgender Sprinters Win 1st and 2nd Place at Connecticut Girls Indoor Track Championships

f **21.3K Share**   🐦 **320 Tweet**   ✉ **Email**

by Cristina Laila

February 24, 2019   758 Comments

Connecticut transgender sprinters won 1st and 2nd place at the state indoor track championships.

In other words, biological males competed against girls and won because they have higher bone density, larger muscles and higher testosterone levels than their biological female opponents.

Connecticut is one of 17 states that allows transgender athletes to compete without any type of restrictions – it's open season and high school girls are the ones suffering because of this insanity.

The Washington Times **reported**:

> ***Yearwood***, *a 17-year-old junior at Cromwell High School, is one of two transgender high school sprinters in Connecticut, transitioning to female.*

GATEWAY PUNDIT

We report the truth — and leave the Russia-Collusion fairy tale to the Conspiracy media

More Accurate than The New York Times, Washington Post, CNN and MSNBC for Two Years and Counting!

Trump-Hating Actor Wears 'Tuxedo Gown' on Oscars Red Carpet to 'Resist Trump' (VIDEO)

f 19.7K Share   🐦 154 Tweet   ✉ Email

by Cristina Laila

February 24, 2019   1039 Comments

Trump-hating, 'gender-fluid' actor, Billy Porter, wears 'tuxedo gown' on Oscar's red carpet to 'resist Trump.'

FINANCIAL TYRANNY-> Chase Bank Shuts Down Personal Account of Vocal Trump-Supporting US Army Combat Vet

f 19.1K Share   🐦 386 Tweet   ✉

by Cristina Laila   February 16, 2019   514 Comments

@RamboBiggs
Joe Biggs

Chase Bank abruptly closed the personal account of US Army combat veteran Joe "Rambo" Biggs.

Mr. Biggs is a very vocal Trump supporter with a bluecheck verified Twitter account and has over 200,000 followers.

"Chase bank just closed out my account!" Biggs said on Twitter Saturday.

> 66 *Chase bank just closed out my account!*
>
>   – Joe Biggs (@Rambobiggs) **February 16, 2019**

Joe Biggs told *The Gateway Pundit* that he was in financial good standing with Chase Bank and had an account with them for almost 20 years.

"I've had my account with Chase since around the year 2000," Biggs said.

Chase Bank sent Mr. Biggs an email letting him know his account had been permanently closed.

The "Green New Deal":
A Radical Mandate for Government Control of American Society

Incoming New York Rep. Alexandria Ocasio-Cortez (left) brings with her a massive online following, influence she says she'll deploy only in support of candidates and politicians who support her plan for a "Green New Deal."

The "Green New Deal" is something Ocasio-Cortez invokes frequently in media appearances and rallies. So what's actually in it? Her office recently released the text of a proposed House rules change outlining the plan.

The proposed rule change for the upcoming 116th Congress would require the creation of a "Select Committee for a Green Deal" that would be responsible for creating the plan by January 1, 2020, with corresponding draft legislation soon after. The text of the rule change lays out the committee's jurisdiction and required areas of action.

Its scope and mandate for legislative authority amounts to a radical grant of power to Washington over Americans' lives, homes, businesses, travel, banking, and more.

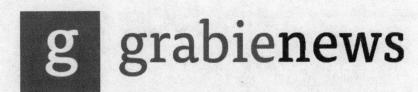

THE 'GREEN NEW DEAL': A RADICAL MANDATE FOR GOVERNMENT CONTROL OF AMERICAN SOCIETY

'Ocasio-Cortez sees this plan is being a vehicle through which social equality might finally realized, as it will use reparations to right historical injustices'

Jan 2, 2019 9:12 PM   G+

By Tom Elliott

Incoming New York Rep. Alexandria Ocasio-Cortez brings with her a massive online following, influence she says she'll deploy only in support of candidates and politicians who support her plan for a "Green New Deal."

"The Green New Deal" is something Ocasio-Cortez invokes frequently in media appearances and rallies.

So what's actually in it?

Her office recently released the text of a proposed House rules change outlining the plan.

The proposed rule change for the upcoming 116th Congress would require the creation of a "Select Committee for a Green Deal" that would be responsible for creating the plan by January 1, 2020, with corresponding draft legislation soon after. The text of the rule change lays out the committee's jurisdiction and required areas of action.

Its scope and mandate for legislative authority amounts to a radical grant of power to Washington over Americans' lives, homes, businesses, travel, banking, and more.

EXCLUSIVE: Calif. college calls the POLICE...over a cartoon frog

Katie Anderson
Colorado Campus Correspondent
@the_katie_joy

Today at 7:25 AM EDT

- Folsom Lake College reported a poster of a cartoon frog to the local police department.

- School leaders wrote an email to students, declaring that "hate has no home on our campus."

Folsom Lake College notified the local police after finding a poster of a cartoon frog, stating that "hate has no home on our campus."

FLORIDA MEN ACCUSED OF PLOT TO GROOM AND RAPE 3-YEAR-OLD GIRL

| f 12,493 | ✉ EMAIL | 👾 SHARE | 🐦 TWEET |

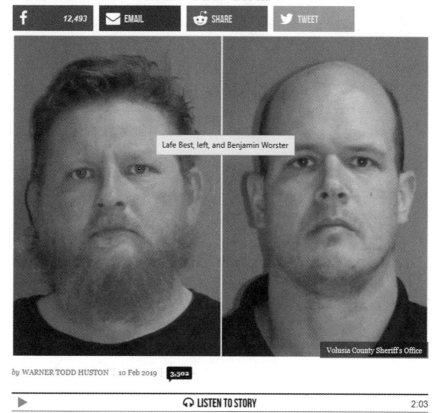

Lafe Best, left, and Benjamin Worster

Volusia County Sheriff's Office

by WARNER TODD HUSTON | 10 Feb 2019 | 💬 3,502

▶ 🎧 LISTEN TO STORY 2:03

Two Florida men have been arrested and charged with plotting to groom and rape a three-year-old girl, a report says.

Police arrested Lafe Best, 37, and Benjamin Worster, 39, after an investigation found the pair planned the alleged plot via texts, according to Tribune Media Wire.

The suspect's plan was first discovered by the potential victim's mother when she saw the text messages on Worster's phone after she found him suffering an apparent drug overdose in her apartment. The woman told police that after she called emergency services for the overdose, she saw Worster's phone. When she began looking through it, she stumbled across the text messages detailing plans to rape her daughter. The woman also told police the girl said Worster had touched her inappropriately at least once.

After an investigation, the Volusia County Sheriff's Office found a series of texts between Worster and his sexual partner, Best, detailing an alleged step-by-step plan to get the child used to seeing them naked, to be comfortable watching pornographic movies, and to being around the two men without others present. The pair also reportedly were searching for a substance that could "knock out" the girl without leaving a trace or harming her.

POPE FRANCIS: CHRISTIANITY AND ISLAM PROTECT 'COMMON VALUES'

The Associated Press

by THOMAS D. WILLIAMS, PH.D.   6 Feb 2019   1,035

 ⌒ LISTEN TO STORY   2:59

Christianity and Islam have more in common than people think, Pope Francis said Wednesday, and the two religions defend common values that are necessary for the future of civilization.

"Despite the diversity of cultures and traditions, the Christian and Islamic worlds appreciate and protect common values: life, family, religious sense, honor for the elderly, the education of the young, and others as well," the pope told the crowds gathered in Saint Peter's Square for his weekly general audience.

The pontiff devoted his weekly address to recapping highlights from his recent three-day trip to the United Arab Emirates, the first visit ever from a pope to the Arabian Peninsula, the birthplace of Islam.

"In an era like our own," Francis said, "in which the temptation is strong to see a clash between the Christian and Islamic civilizations and to consider religions as sources of conflict, we wanted to give a clear and decisive sign, that it is possible to come together, to respect one another and to dialogue."

WND

'MACABRE' BABY BODY-PARTS EXPERIMENTS CONFIRMED

Documents reveal organs of unborn fused to lab rodents

Published: 02/06/2019 at 8:53 PM

| f Share on Facebook | 🐦 Share on Twitter | ✉ Email | ➕ 109 | 🖨 Print | A A |

"Macabre" baby body parts experiments in the United States have been confirmed, according to the Sun newspaper of London.

They involve "grafting dead fetus parts onto mice which are then used to test drugs."

The Sun Online reported it has viewed documents that outline procedures such as cutting out glands and livers of unborn children and fusing them onto lab rodents.

WND reported this week the American Center for Law and Justice is seeking documents from the National Institute of Allergy and Infectious Disease on its "humanized mice" program.

"First, the creation of mice with human immune systems is horrific enough, but that these mice are being created using the body parts of innocent babies is unthinkable," the organization said.

The group cited reports from just months ago detailing "the incredibly disturbing experimentation currently being conducted by the National Institutes of Health (NIH): Using the body parts of aborted babies, the NIH is creating 'humanized mice' for 'HIV therapeutics development.'"

The Sun reported abortion clinics have been supplying researchers in the United States with terminated fetuses.

The Washington Times

Reliable Reporting. The Right Opinion.

Michael Savage, facing death threats, heads to secret location

Talk radio host Michael Savage does not mince words in his 26th book, titled "Stop Mass Hysteria: America's Insanity from the Salem Witch Trials to the Trump Witch Hunt," which will be published Oct. 9. (Courtesy of Center Street Books)
more >

By Cheryl K. Chumley - The Washington Times - Wednesday, January 2, 2019

ANALYSIS/OPINION:

City, state and federal agencies are taking a look at a vicious, hateful email sent a restaurant frequented by talk radio icon Michael Savage that threatens to shoot up the establishment if he's not denied future service.

Remember back in November when Fox News host Tucker Carlson and his family were targeted and threatened by protesters? This is worse.

Portions of the email sent to the restaurant state, in all caps, "I DEMAND THAT YOU REFUSE TO ALLOW MICHAEL SAVAGE … IN YOUR F-ING RESTAURANT AGAIN. HE IS A RACIST WHITE SUPREMACIST PIECE OF SH— … DONT WANT TO LISTEN TO ME? WELL I GUESS YOURE ALL GONNA F—ING DIE THEN CUZ I AM WAITING FOR THE MOTHAF— AND I WILL WAIT AND

Popular talk show host Michael Savage, the victim of death threats, was forced to hide out in a secret location. Across America, the "Deplorables," the middle and working class who support President Donald Trump, have been beaten and their property threatened.

GATEWAY PUNDIT

We report the truth — and leave the Russia-Collusion fairy tale to the Conspiracy media

More Accurate than The New York Times, Washington Post, CNN and MSNBC for Two Years and Counting!

MUST SEE: Footage of Shirtless Bernie Sanders in the USSR Drunkenly Singing with Communists in 1988 Surfaces

f 15.3K Share   y 314 Tweet   ✉ Email

by Cristina Laila

Burlington Soviet Trip 06/13/1988

Footage of a shirtless, drunk Bernie Sanders in the USSR on his 'honeymoon' singing with presumed Soviets in 1988 surfaced and was posted to Twitter on Monday.

The video of Bernie was posted to Twitter by Travis Justin, a Navy veteran and leader of "Draft Beto 2020."

TRAVIS JUSTIN-> NEW: Recently discovered footage from 1988 reveals a shirtless Bernie Sanders with his wife, Jane,

ROB LOWE SLAMS IDIOTIC COLLEGE THAT BANNED PLEDGE OF ALLEGIANCE OVER CONNECTION TO 'WHITE NATIONALISM'

1,175

by JUSTIN CARUSO : 31 Jan 2019   354

▶   ⌔ LISTEN TO STORY   1:22

Actor Rob Lowe slammed the Santa Barbara City College Wednesday following a decision from the Board of Trustees to remove the Pledge of Allegiance from their meetings.

"Humiliated for Santa Barbara City College making national news for their idiocy," Rob Lowe said in a social media post.

 Rob Lowe
@RobLowe

Humiliated for Santa Barbara City College making national news for their idiocy.

GATEWAY PUNDIT

We report the truth — and leave the Russia-Collusion fairy tale to the Conspiracy media

Virginia House Majority Leader Discusses Democrat Bill to Snuff Out a Baby's Life During Birth (VIDEO)

 by Jim Hoft   January 31, 2019   139 Comments

VA GOV SPARKS UPROAR OVER ABORTION COMMENTS

FOX & friends

The plan promoted by the Democrat Party is the most radical law of its kind in the world today.

Gilbert discussed with FOX and Friends his concerns in dealing with Democrats like Delegate Kathy Tran who submitted the barbaric legislation.

Gilbert: ...that she has physical signs that she is about to give birth.

Gilbert reminded the FOX and Friends panel that Tran has four children.
He is understandably worried what Democrats may do if they take control of the Virginia House.

NOLTE: EXPERTS CLAIM EVERY KIND OF WEATHER PROVES GLOBAL WARMING IS FER' REAL

23,278

Christopher Furlong/Getty Images File

by JOHN NOLTE   30 Jan 2019 

▶   ⌒ LISTEN TO STORY   4:26

America enjoys a winter filled with tons of snow and frigid cold weather and out pops the Climate Hoaxsters to assure this kind of weather only further proves our planet is getting, uhm... warmer.

This current Climate Hoaxster freak out is largely in reaction to President Trump's tweet earlier this week mocking the Climate Hoaxsters.

"In the beautiful Midwest, windchill temperatures are reaching minus 60 degrees, the coldest ever recorded," he tweeted. "What the hell is going on with Global Warming? Please come back fast, we need you!"

Donald J. Trump
@realDonaldTrump

In the beautiful Midwest, windchill temperatures are reaching minus 60 degrees, the coldest ever recorded. In coming days, expected to get even colder. People can't last outside even for minutes. What f 337k   y 62.9k   🔖 📷   NEWSLETTER SIGNUP   ◀

COLUMNISTS   NEWSLETTERS   INSTAPUNDIT

NEWS & POLITICS   TRENDING   HOMELAND SECURITY   FAITH   LIFESTYLE   🔍

PARENTING

Dads Dressing in Drag 'For the Children' Is Not Good Parenting

BY MEGAN FOX JANUARY 28, 2019

 Press play to listen to this article
🤖 8:43

I hate 2019. Everywhere I look lately, some bearded, tattooed, or man-bunned millennial dad is dressing up in a princess dress to dance around with his son or daughter while someone videos it. Then that video shows up in my Facebook feed, where every single person on earth feels the need to respond with, "Oh, how adorable!" or "What a good father!" while I just want to pull out my hair and scream *WHAT THE HELL IS WRONG WITH EVERYONE AND WHERE IS THE WHISKEY?*

I have three major problems with this:

1. Dressing in drag with your son is not a kindness to him.

If your son wants to wear princess dresses, he has one of two issues. The first is very simple and about 99.9 percent of cross-dressing toddlers fall into this category. *He wants a cool costume.* That's it. There's no hidden message, but girls have way cooler things to dress up in than boys, unless you go out looking for them online or make them yourself. My son wanted to wear a princess dress once because he has two sisters and they have a closet full of them and let's face it, they're sparkly and fabulous. What kid doesn't want to be a part of dress-up?

That was the moment I could have been one of those moms who overreacts and puts her 3-year-old son in a dress and starts calling him "Maizy" and forces the neighbors to say "she." But I didn't do that. Instead, I pulled out my sewing machine

🅑 BREITBART

PETE DAVIDSON ENRAGES AUDIENCE WITH JOKES ABOUT HAVING SEX WITH A BABY

558

by JEROME HUDSON ⋮ 28 Jan 2019 ⋮ 911

▶   🎧 LISTEN TO STORY   1:51

Actor Pete Davidson reportedly left audience members angry last week during a shocking comedy set that saw the *Saturday Night Live* star cracking jokes about having sex with his friend's baby.

At one point during his routine at The Bell House in Brooklyn, New York, Davidson relayed a story about the time he was babysitting his friend's child. The baby was teething. Davidson noticed the baby sucking his finger, but in "good" way he quipped.

"I don't want to fuck this baby but he's asking for it," Davidson said, according to the Montreal Gazette. He later added that he's not into having sex with babies but if he was, he would choose that baby.

Breitbart TV

AMY SCHUMER SHARES 'HORRIFYING' VAGINA BABY SHOWER CAKE

5,375

by WARNER TODD HUSTON   28 Jan 2019   3,777

Comedienne and actress Amy Schumer looked shocked by the "horrifying" baby shower cake replete with a "butthole" that featured a baby's face emerging from a birth canal given to her by her sister-in-law.

Amy Schumer jumped to her Instagram account to post a series of photos of the raunchy cake made to look like a woman giving birth.

"My sister in law. And I can't stress that enough IN LAW. surprised me with a horrifying cake and i can't thank her enough," Schumer wrote.

Daily Mail.com

Pop songs have become angrier AND sadder! Scientists analysed lyrics from 6,000 best-selling songs from the 1950s to 2016 to make the finding

- Study was by experts from Lawrence Technological University in Michigan
- They looked at lyrics from more than 6,000 songs from the US Billboard Hot 100
- Songs released during the mid 1950s were the least angry and the most upbeat

By TIM COLLINS FOR MAILONLINE
PUBLISHED: 12:04 EDT, 25 January 2019 | UPDATED: 12:07 EDT, 25 January 2019

Pop songs have become angrier and sadder over the past 60 years, experts say.

Researchers analysed lyrics in best-selling songs from the 1950s to 2016 to find expressions of anger and sadness had increased, while words about joy had dropped.

The US study team looked at lyrics of more than 6,000 songs from Billboard Hot 100 in each year.

These are the most popular songs in the US each year as chosen by music fans.

In the past songs were ranked mainly by record sales, radio and jukebox plays, but more recently it is based on other popularity indicators such as streaming and social media to reflect changes in music consumption.

Tones expressed in each song were analysed using 'automatic quantitative sentiment' which looked at each word or phrase in the song with a set of tones they express.

The combination of the tones expressed by all words and phrases of the lyrics determines the sentiment of that song.

The sentiments of all Billboard Hot 100 songs in each year are averaged and the average of each year measured whether the expression of that sentiment increased, decreased or remained the same.

The analysis showed the expression of anger in popular music lyrics has increased gradually over time.

Study co-author Lior Shamir, of Lawrence Technological University in Michigan, said: 'The change in lyrics sentiments does not necessarily reflect what the musicians and songwriters wanted to express, but is more related to what music consumers wanted to listen to in each year.'

The US study team looked at lyrics of more than 6,000 songs from Billboard Hot 100 in each year. These are the most popular songs in the US each year as chosen by music fans. Songs released during the mid 1950s, like those of Buddy Holly (left) were the least angry. More recent music like Adele's (right) contain more lyrics dealing with sadness

SOCIETY COMMENTARY

'I Have a Girl Brain but a Boy Body': Virginia Kindergartners Are Read Transgender Story

Tony Perkins / @tperkins / March 06, 2019

💬 COMMENTARY BY

Tony Perkins @tperkins

Tony Perkins is president of the Family Research Council.

It looked like your typical reading class. Dozens of kindergarten students sat cross-legged on the floor watching their teacher turn to the first page. It didn't take long for the 5-year-olds to realize: This was no ordinary children's book. "I have a girl brain but a boy body," Miss McBride started. "This is called transgender. I was born this way."

Thanks to a new partnership between two radically liberal forces—the National Education Association and Human Rights Campaign—there's no telling how many elementary school students heard the exact same message in their own classrooms. That's because Monday was Read Across America Day, and for the first time, the country's biggest LGBT extremists were official sponsors.

The NEA, which has been a satellite office for the far-left wing of the Democratic Party for years, insisted that it was "urgent" to ally with HRC now that the president has rolled back Barack Obama's bathroom mandate. "The Trump administration has been openly hostile," said NEA President Lily Garcia, "whether or not you're a transgender soldier or transgender little boy or girl. It is more important than ever before that we speak out."

In The Washington Post article about this new initiative, no one explains whether parents were warned. Judging by both organizations' track record, it's safe to assume they weren't. After all, this is exactly the kind of outrageous indoctrination that's caused millions of parents to pull their kids out of school and either move them to Christian campuses or teach them at home.

Houston Public Library

Drag Queen Storytime

SATURDAY, SEPTEMBER 30
1:00-1:45 PM

Break out the dress-up chest and let your imagination run wild!

Featuring: Blackberri and Tatiana Mala-Niña Hosted by Space Kiddettes

Freed-Montrose Library
Houston. TX 77006

houstonlibrary.org
832-393-1800

Grotesque Drag Queen reads to kids at story time at the Michelle Obama Library in Long Beach, California.

CHRISTIAN HEADLINES

Topics Blog Slideshows Columnists Contributors Subscribe About

HOT TOPICS   #christian persecution   #church   #LGBT   #politics   #Mike Pence

Elementary Schools Using Drag Queens to Teach Kids about Gender

Scott Slayton | *Contributor to ChristianHeadlines.com* | Wednesday, August 8, 2018

1K 🐦 Tweet   #education   #top headlines   #LGBT   #transgender
📘 Share

3   Some teachers and schools have utilized a program called "Drag Queen Story
Comments   Hour" to teach children about gender identity.

🖨 Print ✉ Email   Videographer Sean Fitzgerald and the David Horowitz Freedom Center
                     released a video explaining the program and highlighting testimonials on the
program's website from teachers in public schools. Fitzgerald drew attention to this issue, not
because of the existence of the program, but because public schools have used it to teach
children about gender issues at a tender age.

On its website, the Drag Queen Story Hour describes itself as, "drag queens reading stories to
children in libraries, schools, and bookstores. DQSH captures the imagination and play of the
gender fluidity of childhood and gives kids glamorous, positive, and unabashedly queer role
models. In spaces like this, kids are able to see people who defy rigid gender restrictions and
imagine a world where people can present as they wish, where dress up is real."

The New York Times described one of the events, hosted by a branch of the New York Public
Library, in 2017. A six-foot-tall performer named "Harmonica Sunbeam," wearing a neon
camouflage bodysuit and a purple tutu read to the children. She read "from 'Morris Micklewhite
and the Tangerine Dress' by Christine Baldacchino. The book is about a boy who wore a beloved
dress to school every day. At one point, Morris's friends inform him that he isn't allowed to play
on their imaginary spaceship, because 'astronauts can't wear dresses.'"

Her recommendation says, "What an amazing way to teach about individuality, empathy, and
acceptance! Drag Queen Story Hour gave my first graders a fun and interactive platform to talk
and think about social and emotional issues like acceptance, being yourself, and loving who you
are…During our debrief after DQSH, they were preaching the incredible lessons they had learned
like 'It's ok to be different,' and 'There's no such thing as 'boy' things and 'girl' things." She
added that she looks forward to hosting another event next year.

Fitzgerald noted his issue with the story hour taking place in public schools, saying, "The
taxpayer is funding adult-themed performers to come and read to our smallish children in order
to indoctrinate them into a political ideology about gender while, at the same time, school
districts across the country are removing any and all references to biological sex from science
textbooks."

The Drag Queen Story Hour was founded in 2014 and now has chapters in twenty states and
the United Kingdom.

Home   About   Privacy   Advertise   Store   Search

GATEWAY PUNDIT

We report the truth — and leave the Russia-Collusion fairy tale to the Conspiracy media

More Accurate than The New York Times, Washington Post, CNN and MSNBC for Two Years and Counting!

Child Abuse? 10-Year-old Boy Dressed in 'Drag' Photographed With Nude Adult Male 'Drag Queen'

f 725 Share   🐦 181 Tweet   ✉ Email

by Cristina Laila   January 14, 2019   413 Comments

Queen Lactatia at Drag Con 2017, screen image via YouTube

Last week, a 10-year-old boy dressed in drag was photographed with a naked adult male 'drag queen.'

A 10-year-old Canadian boy, Nemis Quinn Mélançon-Golden who goes by the stage name 'Queen Lactatia' was **featured** in an appalling piece in Huck Magazine titled, 'Queen Lactatia: What Life is Like as a Child Drag Queen.'

The child was photographed in several different dresses and wigs with a full face of dramatic makeup on – one photograph didn't make Huck Magazine, but it made its way to Instagram.

The photographer, Jonathan Frederick Turton, posted a photograph of Nemis, a prepubescent boy, posing with a nude adult male drag queen named 'Violet Chachki' to his **Instagram** account.

Violet Chachki is a male 'drag queen' and winner of Season 7 of "RuPaul's Drag Race."

The Instagram post has since been deleted, however, the child is seen dressed in drag standing next to Violet Chachki, an adult male with a tiny piece of cloth covering his genitals.

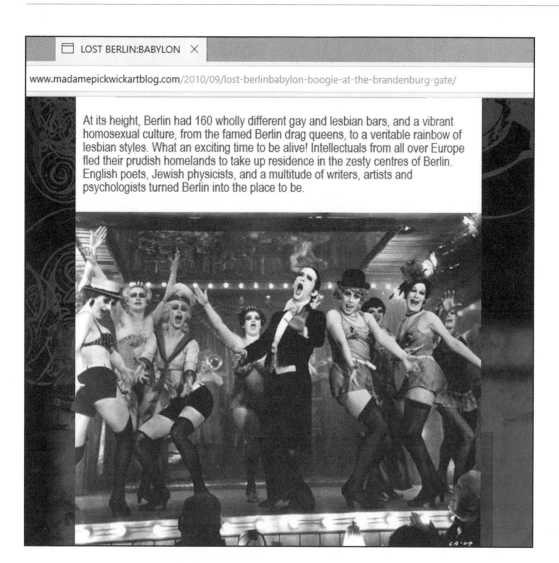

LOST BERLIN:BABYLON ✕

www.madamepickwickartblog.com/2010/09/lost-berlinbabylon-boogie-at-the-brandenburg-gate/

At its height, Berlin had 160 wholly different gay and lesbian bars, and a vibrant homosexual culture, from the famed Berlin drag queens, to a veritable rainbow of lesbian styles. What an exciting time to be alive! Intellectuals from all over Europe fled their prudish homelands to take up residence in the zesty centres of Berlin. English poets, Jewish physicists, and a multitude of writers, artists and psychologists turned Berlin into the place to be.

Jim Hoft ✓
@gatewaypundit

Follow ⌄

Leftwing Nutcase @Cher Calls for All Men to be Circumcised and Show Papers or Penis
thegatewaypundit.com/2019/03/leftwi... via @gatewaypundit

Leftwing Nutcase Cher Calls for All Men to be Circumcised and Show Papers...
The last few weeks radical Democrat freshmen made headlines for their radical, dangerous ideas and offensive, anti-Semitic ramblings. On Monday singer-actress...
thegatewaypundit.com

Jim Hoft ✓
@gatewaypundit

Writer- Speaker- Where Hope Made a Comeback - Top Choice of the American Truth Seeker

GALLUP: SOCIALISM BECOMING NORMALIZED AMONG DEMOCRATS

9,771

by ALANA MASTRANGELO ┆ 6 Jan 2019 ┆ 4,666

▶   ∩ LISTEN TO STORY   2:24

Socialism is becoming more normalized among Americans who identify as Democrats, according to a recent poll, as their approval of capitalism falls at the same time.

A recent Gallup poll showed that 57 percent of Democrats view socialism positively, while 47 percent of Democrats view capitalism positively. Across the aisle, only 16 percent of Republicans view socialism in a positive light, a number still frighteningly high among those who identify as conservative.

The Gallup poll adds that the youth are more likely to favor socialism than those who are older. "Evidence for this is found in the strong support younger voters gave Bernie Sanders during his 2016 presidential campaign," says Gallup, "and in the candidacy of Ocasio-Cortez."

Socialists — running for office as democrats — are indeed getting elected, as they promise to provide young Americans with free services, in which they will make other generations pay for.

At left is a picture of the Democratic Congresswomen and Senators at the 2018 State of the Union Address by President Trump. At right is the Photoshop version.

Two popular models related to the Democratic Party's fashion styles—at left a transgender and at right, an obese swimmer. Their intent is to change American culture.

ABORTION LEADING CAUSE OF DEATH IN 2018 WITH 41 MILLION KILLED

99,366

Scott Olson/Getty Images

by THOMAS D. WILLIAMS, PH.D. | 31 Dec 2018 14,000

▶ 🎧 LISTEN TO STORY 2:53

Abortion was the number one cause of death worldwide in 2018, with more than 41 million children killed before birth, Worldometers reports.

As of December 31, 2018, there have been some 41.9 million abortions performed in the course of the year, Worldometers revealed. By contrast, 8.2 million people died from cancer in 2018, 5 million from smoking, and 1.7 million died of HIV/AIDS.

Worldometers — voted one of the best free reference websites by the American Library Association (ALA) — keeps a running tally through the year of major world statistics, including population, births, deaths, automobiles produced, books published, and CO2 emissions.

CHUCK TODD DEDICATES SUNDAY'S 'MEET THE PRESS' TO 'CLIMATE CRISIS,' BANS 'CLIMATE DENIERS' FROM SHOW

15,418

❚❚ ↺ 🔊 00:01 / 06:37 ⚙ ⤢

by TRENT BAKER : 30 Dec 2018 [7,880]

▶ 🎧 **LISTEN TO STORY** 1:14

Sunday, NBC's "Meet the Press" host Chuck Todd dedicated his final show of the year to the "climate crisis," which he said has "been ignored for far too long."

Todd also announced he would not "give time to climate deniers," declaring "the science is settled."

"The evidence is everywhere," the host said as a voice-over on the show's lead-in that included clips of nasty weather and Sen. Liz Warren (D-MA) declaring climate change's authenticity and danger.

"Just as important as what we are going to do this hour is what we're not going to do," Todd opened. "We're not going to debate climate change, the existence of it. The Earth is getting hotter. And human activity is a major cause, period. We're not going to give time to climate deniers. The science is settled, even if political opinion is not."

Instead of "climate deniers," Todd brought former New York City Mayor Michael Bloomberg, climate scientist Kate Marvel and Democratic California Governor Jerry Brown on the show to discuss climate change.

Follow Trent Baker on Twitter @MagnifiTrent

Home   About   Privacy   Advertise   Store   f 🐦   Search

GATEWAY PUNDIT

We report the truth — and leave the Russia-Collusion fairy tale to the Conspiracy media

More Accurate than The New York Times, Washington Post, CNN and MSNBC for Two Years and Counting!

Facebook Eliminated Over One Billion Page-Views to Conservative Websites from 2017 to 2018 – Now, Thanks to James O'Keefe, We Have Proof This Was The Plan

 by Jim Hoft   February 27, 2019   195 Comments

f 19.7K Share   🐦 442 Tweet   ✉ Email

Facebook has been shutting down traffic to conservative websites since the 2016 election.

Conservatives dominated social media in 2016 where they were able to get the truth uncensored. Facebook ended that in 2017 and 2018.

The Gateway Pundit spoke with two of the top conservative publishers in America.

Floyd Brown is a conservative author, speaker and media commentator. In 2008 Floyd launched **Western Journal** which quickly became one of the top conservative websites in America. By 2016 Floyd's organization of Western Journal and other conservative websites under his umbrella had more than a billion page views. **Since 2016 Floyd's organization lost 75% of its Facebook traffic.**

Likewise, we spoke with **Jared Vallorani** from **Klicked Media**. Jared traveled to Washington DC with The Gateway Pundit and website owners at **100%FedUp** in June to discuss Facebook targeting against conservative publishers with Republican lawmakers. Jared told The Gateway Pundit his organization Klicked Media, which hosts over 60 conservative websites, **lost 400 million page views from Facebook in the last six months if you compare the traffic to a year ago.** Jared said, "We lost 70% to 80% of our traffic if you compare January to May 2017 vs Jan to May 2018."

If you combine the total number of page-views lost by just these two conservative online publishers you are looking at a loss of over 1.5 billion page-views from Facebook in one year.

These are numbers from just two of the top conservative publishers in America. This does not include the thousands of other conservative publishers across the country who lost all of their traffic coming from Facebook. Here at The Gateway Pundit our Facebook traffic has been effectively eliminated after we were ranked as the 4th most influential conservative publisher in the 2016 election.

The fact that Facebook is targeting conservative publishers should not be a surprise to Gateway Pundit readers.

We have been reporting on this for several months now. In July we released a study where we looked at several top conservative websites and discovered that the publishers had **lost an average of 93%** of their Facebook traffic.

WHEN THE EXACT SAME GROUP OF "EXPERTS" WHO CLAIMED IT WAS GLOBAL COOLING IN 1977

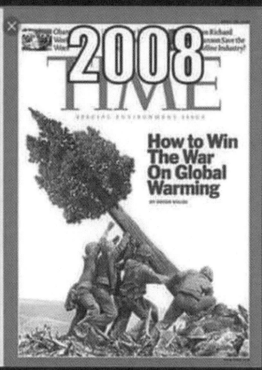

NOW CLAIM IT'S GLOBAL WARMING YOU CAN EASILY SEE WHY I AM SKEPTICAL

California Congressman Ted Lieu at LGBT parade.

COLUMNISTS NEWSLETTERS INSTAPUNDIT

NEWS & POLITICS   TRENDING   HOMELAND SECURITY   FAITH   LIFESTYLE

TRENDING

Chicago Elects First Black Female Lesbian Mayor as Socialists Gain

 BY RICK MORAN APRIL 3, 2019 💬 145 COMMENTS

Lori Lightfoot speaks at her election night party Tuesday, April 2, 2019, in Chicago. Lori Lightfoot elected Chicago mayor, making her the first African-American woman to lead the city. (AP Photo/Nam Y. Huh)

Former prosecutor Lori Lightfoot rode a wave of disgust at corruption in city hall to coast to victory in Chicago's mayoral race. She becomes the first black female mayor in the city's history.

Lightfoot easily bested Cook County Board Commissioner Toni Preckwinkle with nearly 75 percent of the vote. Preckwinkle, a former teacher backed by the unions and the Chicago political establishment, got caught up in the bribery scandal that ensnared long-time Alderman Ed Burke and couldn't get rid of the stench.

For her part, all Lightfoot had to do was prove to voters she was not part of the corrupt political machine that has held sway in the city for 100 years. She bucked city hall two years ago when, as a member of the police board, she drove the investigation into the Laquan McDonald shooting. That gave her profile in the city a boost and she eventually used the incident as a springboard to power.

As all reformers who came before her, Lightfoot promised change.

Fox News:

> Lightfoot promised to rid City Hall of corruption and help low-income and working-class people she said had been "left behind and ignored" by Chicago's political ruling class. It was a message that resonated with voters weary of political scandal and insider deals, and who said the city's leaders for too long have invested in downtown at the expense of neighborhoods.
>
> "Together we can and will make Chicago a place where your zip code doesn't determine your destiny," Lightfoot told a cheering crowd at her victory party. "We can and we will break this city's endless cycle of corruption and never again — never ever — allow politicians to profit from elected positions."
>
> She said people are seeing "a city reborn" — a place where race and "who you love" don't matter.

Winning the mayoral race in Chicago is not exactly like being elected captain of the *Titanic*, but it's close. Lightfoot will face a pension bomb waiting to detonate, out of control gang violence, massive mistrust of police by the black community, crumbling schools, a disappearing tax base, and neighborhoods that resemble war

Daily**Mail**.com

| Home Updated: 14:54 EDT

Home | U.K. | News | Sports | U.S. Showbiz | Australia | Femail | Health | Science

Latest headlines | World News | Books | Horoscopes | Work with Us | Games

Is America becoming Godless? The number of people who have no religion has risen 266 per cent - one third of the population - in three decades

- People with no religion accounted for 23.1% of the U.S. population in 2018
- By comparison, Catholics make up 23% and Evangelicals account for 22.5%
- The three are now statistically tied as the largest religious groups in America
- Meanwhile, mainline Protestant Christianity has seen a 62.5% decline in believers since 1982, to now account for just 10.8% of the U.S. population

By VALERIE BAUMAN SOCIAL AFFAIRS REPORTER FOR DAILYMAIL.COM
PUBLISHED: 10:45 EDT, 4 April 2019 | UPDATED: 06:32 EDT, 6 April 2019

      13k shares **347** View comments

The number of Americans who identify as having no religion has risen 266 percent since 1991, to now tie statistically with the number of Catholics and Evangelicals, according to a new survey.

People with no religion – known as 'nones' among statisticians – account for 23.1 percent of the U.S. population, while Catholics make up 23 percent and Evangelicals account for 22.5 percent, according to the **General Social Survey**.

Those three groups now represent the largest the religious groups in America.

The survey has tracked a broad swath of American trends since 1972, offering comprehensive insight into the evolving face of religion over more than four decades.

Ryan Burge, a political science professor at Eastern Illinois University who analyzed the data, said that experts have several theories about why the number of 'nones' has risen so dramatically in recent decades.

'One of them is that many people used to lie about what they were,' he told DailyMail.com. 'Many people were (always) atheist or non-religious, but it was previously culturally unacceptable to not have a religion in America.'

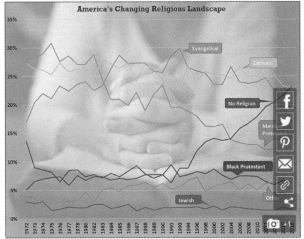

This graph illustrates the shift in religious ideologies since 1972, with a sharp decline in the number of mainline Protestant Christians and a dramatic uptick in the number of people with no religion. Known as 'nones' those religion-free Americans are now statistically tied with Catholics and Evangelicals as the largest religious groups in America

Shifting political ideologies about social issues has also played a role, with fewer

News Podcasts Authors Events Store Login Q

Ocasio-Cortez: People Maybe Shouldn't Reproduce Due To Climate Change

"Is it okay to still have children?"

By RYAN SAAVEDRA
🐦 @REALSAAVEDRA

February 25, 2019

Democratic socialist Rep. Alexandria Ocasio-Cortez (D-NY) suggested on Sunday night that people should consider not having children due to climate change because there is a "scientific consensus" that life will be hard for kids.

"Our planet is going to hit disaster if we don't turn this ship around and so it's basically like, there's a scientific consensus that the lives of children are going to be very difficult," Ocasio-Cortez said while chopping up food in her kitchen during an Instagram live video. "And it does lead, I think, young people to have a legitimate question, you know, 'Is it okay to still have children?'"

Ocasio-Cortez then took a shot at Sen. Dianne Feinstein (D-CA) over an **incident that happened** in Feinstein's office on Friday when a far-left fringe group tried to pressure Feinstein into supporting the Green New Deal.

"You know what's interesting about this group?" Feinstein told the group on Friday, in response to the group storming into her office. "I've been doing this for 30 years. I know what I'm doing."

"You come in here, and you say it has to be my way or the highway. I don't respond to that," Feinstein continued. "I've gotten elected, I just ran. I was elected by almost a million-vote plurality. And I know what I'm doing. So you know, maybe people

in's response was "like not good enough" because the
ats support is "frankly going to kill us."

rking on this for x-amount of years,' um, it's like not
ez said. "Like, we need a universal sense of urgency, and
roduce watered-down proposals that are frankly going
is going to kill us."

Chairman of the Intel Committee in the House, Adam Schiff. Notice his wild eyes.

Democratic Congresswoman Ocasio-Cortez says the world will end by 2030. Notice her wild eyes.

This demonstrator wants to spend more money on Climate Change.

UNIVERSITY OF NORTH TEXAS COURSE TEACHES STUDENTS ABOUT 'SEXUAL PLEASURE' FOR INFANTS

| f 50,152 | ✉ EMAIL | 🔁 SHARE | 🐦 TWEET |

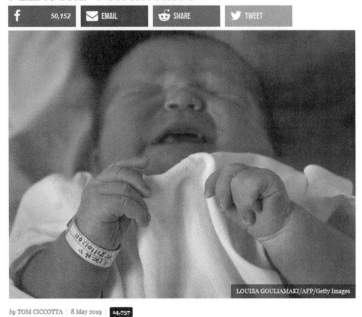

LOUISA GOULIAMAKI/AFP/Getty Images

by TOM CICCOTTA | 8 May 2019 | 14,757

▶ 🎧 LISTEN TO STORY 2:01

A human sexuality course at the University of North Texas asks enrolled students to observe "sexual interactions" in young children. The class also included a presentation titled "Sexual Pleasure and Response in Infants."

A report from The College Fix revealed that a course at the University of North Texas is taking a bizarre stance on the sexuality of young children. The course, which is entitled "Psychology and Sexual Behavior," has been criticized for an alleged lesson on "sexual pleasure" in "infants." Photos from the classroom show a PowerPoint presentation with the title "Sexual Pleasure and Response in Infants."

The College Fix highlighted an excerpt from the course's textbook, which is called *Our Sexuality* asks students to go to a local elementary school playground or daycare center to observe "sexual interactions" between the children.

> Take the class to a local elementary school playground, or ask permission for a few of your students to attend various school playgrounds, preschools, or daycare centers during recess to observe behaviors of children. Ask students to note interactions between same-sex and mixed-sex groups. Which group was more frequent? Which behaviors were most frequent? What kind of touching did children engage in? What about teasing behaviors? Were there any overtly sexual interactions? What was the age range of the children being observed? Have students write a report comparing their observations with information in the text.

The textbook editor told The College Fix that she has never taken students to a local elementary school or daycare center to observe "sexual interactions."

"I can say that as an instructor I have never used that activity and I would be quite surprised if any instructor has asked their students to observe children on a playground."

🅵 337k 🆈 62.9k 🄵 ⊚   NEWSLETTER SIGNUP

COLUMNISTS NEWSLETTERS INSTAPUN

NEWS & POLITICS TRENDING HOMELAND SECURITY FAITH LIFESTYLE

Pennsylvania's First Openly Gay Representative Attacks Elderly Woman Praying in Front of Planned Parenthood

BY MEGAN FOX MAY 6, 2019   💬 739 COMMENTS

Pennsylvania House of Representatives Official Portrait of Representative Brian Sims (D-Philadelphia)

In what can only be described as a gross violation of the code of conduct befitting a member of the Pennsylvania General Assembly, new member Brian Sims (D-Philadelphia) openly harassed an elderly pro-life woman praying outside a Planned Parenthood in his district. Not only did Sims, the first openly (and rabidly) gay representative behave like a threatening bully, but he may have committed a crime. According to the Pennsylvania code, criminal harassment is defined thus:

> **A person commits the crime of harassment when, with intent to harass, annoy or alarm another,** the person: (1) strikes, shoves, kicks or otherwise subjects the other person to physical contact, or attempts or threatens to do the same; (2) **follows the other person in or about a public place or places;**

It seems obvious that Sims' intention was to cha
sidewalk where she was legally allowed to stand

⊙62 CBS Detroit   NEWS WEATHER SPORTS BEST OF VIDEO A

Convicted Child Rapist Vows To 'Rape The First Woman He Sees' After Release

Categories: Content, News, Local News, WWJTV

Officials in Arkansas issued a warning Monday about a level 3 sex offender who threatened to "rape the first woman he sees" after he's released from custody. Matt Yurus reports.

THE COLLEGE FIX

DONATE | SUBSCRIBE

ORIGINAL. STUDENT REPORTED. YOUR DAILY DOSE OF *RIGHT*-MINDED NEWS AND COMMENTARY FROM ACROSS THE NATION.

News ⌄   Student Reporters   Opinion   About The Fix   Write For Us   Contact   🔍

RACIAL ISSUES   RELIGION   WHITE PRIVILEGE

Keynote speaker at Harvard diversity conference says Christians should be 'locked up'

ALEXANDER PEASE - UMASS BOSTON   ·   APRIL 26, 2019

SHARE THIS ARTICLE: (f) (y) (🌐) (✉)

Christians 'deserve to be mocked viciously and run out of the public square'

To celebrate a "Decade of Dialogue" in its annual diversity conference, Harvard University's Faculty of Arts & Sciences invited a straight white man to give the keynote lecture.

From Diversity to Inclusio
10 Years of Dialogue

Over the last ten years, the FAS Diversity Dialog conversation about diversity, equality, and inclusi and beyond. Join us for a retrospective look at th inclusion, and discussion of current issues and p can move toward greater inclusion and belongin

We are pleased to announce that our keynote sp prominent activist, author and educator. In additi conference will include a moderated panel discus and an opportunity to meet colleagues and to lea

Keynote Speaker Tim Wise

Spring, 2019

Register online at www.hr.fas.harvard.edu

But not just any straight white man.

Tim Wise, an "anti-racism writer, educator and activist," has denigrated Christians as "**Jeezoids**" and **fascists** and called Pope Francis **evil**. He has **tweeted** that "people who believe in a God of hell/damnation deserve to be mocked viciously and run out of the public square."

Those who base their morality on the Hebrew Scriptures "deserve to be locked up," **he said in 2015**, claiming to be "sorta kidding but not by much."

The Diversity Dialogue Series provides a "retrospective look at diversity and inclusion, a discussion of current issues, and practical guidance on how we can move toward greater inclusion and belonging at Harvard," according to the **event description**.

Attributes his success to multiple forms of 'privilege'

Wise avoided inflammatory anti-religious language in his keynote, perhaps mindful that the Christians he wants to incarcerate are a racially diverse lot.

The author of "White Like Me: Reflections on Race from a Privileged Son" and "Dear White America: Letter to a New Minority" instead emphasized his own wokeness.

Wise boasted that he had "never been invited to speak by ICE," distinguishing himself from a biracial consultant on the panel discussion before his keynote.

He described his teenage daughter as "militant, straight and cis-gendered ally to the struggle against transphobia, cisnormativity, and heterosexism and heteronormativity." He jokingly asked the audience to pray for him and his wife as their daughter applies to colleges.

The activist emphasized the importance of identifying institutional barriers to diversity and inclusion.

White supremacy does not only exist on a case-by-case basis, but more broadly serves to shape the "superstructure of society," Wise told the audience.

Actress Julia Roberts says every bathroom should be gender neutral and be open to every sex.

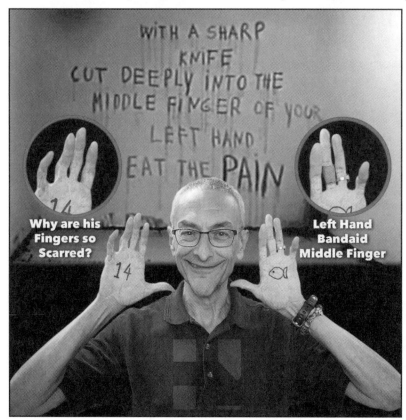

Democrat Party activist, John Podesta, shows off his secret number and symbol. The rough drawn sign at top is the work of Marina Abramovic, a loathsome witch in Progressive circles.

Marina Abramovic with severed goat's head.

●●●○○ Sprint LTE   7:02 PM   ✴ ▭

Q 🔒 marina abramovic art gala   ↻

scrapaduq - WordPress.com

Debbie Harry and her likeness

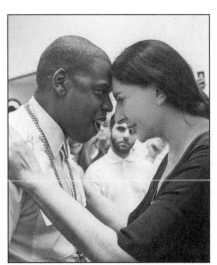

Above, left: Abramovic with bloody bones.

Above, Abramovic, a close friend of Bill and Hillary Clinton's greets Jay-Z, husband of Beyoncé.

Left, Marina Abramovic and actor Robert DeNiro at Abramovic's satanic gala.

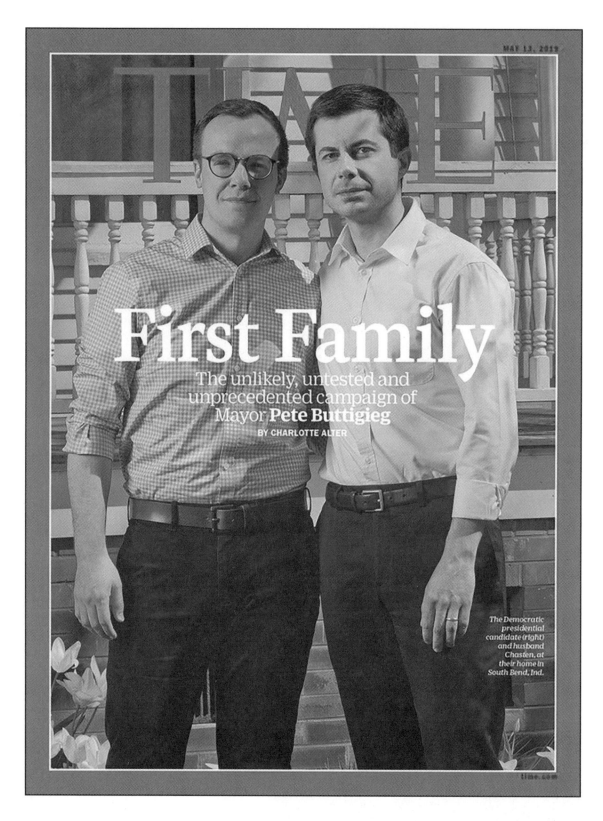

MAY 13, 2019

First Family

The unlikely, untested and
unprecedented campaign of
Mayor **Pete Buttigieg**
BY CHARLOTTE ALTER

The Democratic
presidential
candidate (right)
and husband
Chasten, at
their home in
South Bend, Ind.

time.com

GATEWAY PUNDIT
We report the truth — and leave the Russia-Collusion fairy tale to the Conspiracy media

More Accurate than The New York Times, Washington Post, CNN and MSNBC for Two Years and Counting!

Bloody Decapitated Trump Head on Sword in DC Park Blocks From White House

by Kristinn Taylor   January 23, 2019   268 Comments

f 14.5K Share   🐦 159 Tweet   ✉ Email

A mock bloody, decapitated head of President Trump was put on end of the upraised sword of the Joan of Arc Statue in Meridian Hill Park in Northwest Washington, D.C., last Saturday according to several photographs posted online. The Trump head had red streamers coming down from the base to give the appearance of blood flowing to make clear the message of decapitation of the President.

Meridian Hill Park, also known locally as Malcolm X Park, is **administered by the U.S. Park Service**. The park is located about 15 blocks due north of the White House. The decapitated Trump head was not up all weekend, apparently, but long enough for it to be photographed by several locals.

GA
We report the

More Accurate than The New York Times, Washington Post, CNN and MSNBC for Two Years and Counting!

Satan's Party: Congressional Democrats on Committee Propose Removing "So Help You God" From Oath

by Jim Hoft   January 29, 2019   279 Comments

f 14.4K Share   🐦 314 Tweet   ✉ Email

At the 2012 DNC Convention Democrats booed God and Israel.

Democrats on the House Committee on Natural Resources proposed to remove the words "so help you God" from the oath recited before committee hearings.

They find it offensive.

The Hill reported:

> The House Committee on Natural Resources is reportedly seeking to have the words "so help you God" removed from the oath recited by witnesses who testify before the panel, according to a proposal obtained by Fox News.
>
> The rules proposal states that witnesses appearing in hearings before the committee would be administered the following oath: "Do you solemnly swear or affirm, under penalty of law, that the testimony that you are about to give is the truth, the whole truth, and nothing but the truth[, so help you God]?"
>
> According to Fox News, the "so help you God" phrasing is written in brackets in red in the draft which indicates the words are slated for removal.

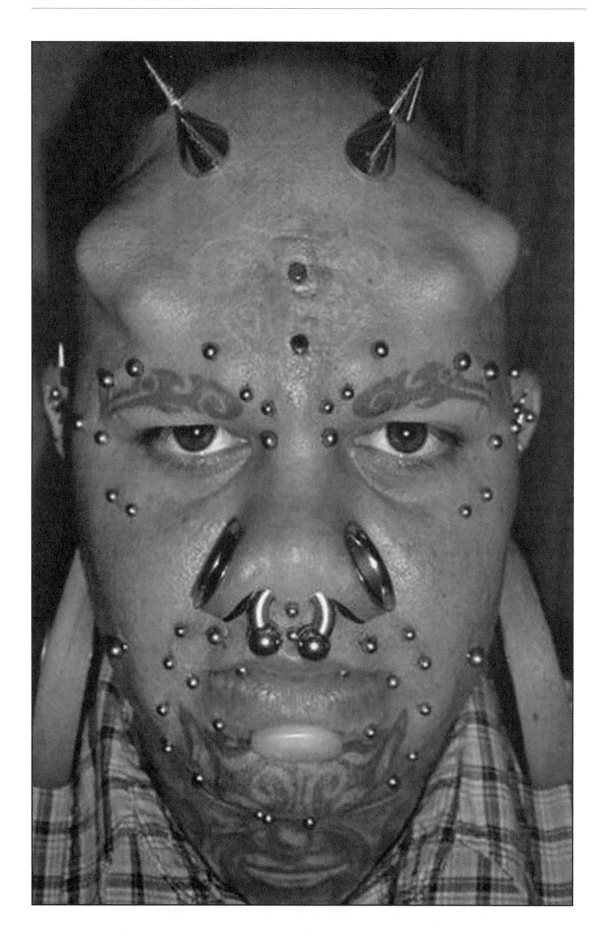

A young Anderson Cooper, with brother Carter and mother, Gloria Vanderbilt, at home in bed. Observe the Witchcraft Queen artwork on the wall.

▶ Q !ITPb.qbhqo 12/13/17 (Wed) 23:24:04 ID: 3610ff No.93181
File (hide): 026fc3e1d6bb5bb···.jpeg (67.35 KB, 480x480, 1:1, 7803B61A-1F3E-47BD-88D4-F....jpeg) (h) (u)

Saw this in last thread.
Focus on papers on table.
Graphic at top.
They all belong to the same sick cult/club.
Q

CNN's Anderson Cooper. Note the odd doll. Is this a depiction of the murdered Jon Benet Ramsey?

Infowars.com took this photo of a crazed stalker.

🅱 BREITBART

HULU SERIES 'SHRILL' COLLABORATES WITH PLANNED PARENTHOOD: GETTING AN ABORTION MAKES YOU FEEL 'REALLY GOOD' AND 'F*CKING POWERFUL'

| f | 16,426 | ✉ EMAIL | 🔴 SHARE | 🐦 TWEET |

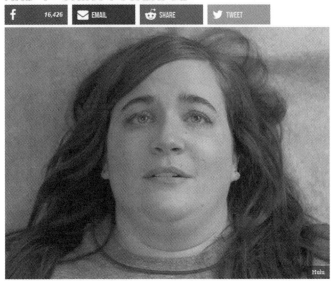

Hulu

by JUSTIN CARUSO | 18 Mar 2019 | **5,613**

In an episode from the Hulu series "Shrill," the main character Annie has an abortion and later declares that her decision made her feel "really, really good."

As first reported by MRC's Newsbusters, the new Hulu series is about an "overweight journalist" named Annie, played by Aidy Bryant, known for her role on *Saturday Night Live*.

In the episode, Annie has unprotected sex with a man she's been seeing, and takes a morning after pill. However, the pill fails because of how overweight she is, leaving her pregnant.

She eventually decides to get an abortion, which is quick and painless. Planned Parenthood actually worked with the show to "[depict] sexual reproductive health care accurately."

Finally, after Annie rests post-abortion, she tells her roommate that she now feels "really, really good" and "very fucking powerful."

Hulu has featured a number of shows with political messages over the last few years.

The growing streaming service picked up Sarah Silverman's commentary show *I Love You, America*, which featured plenty of political posturing, such as when Silverman compared President Donald Trump to Adolf Hitler in October. *I Love You, America* was later cancelled after only 21 episodes.

Hulu is also home to the series *Handmaid's Tale*, which depicts a society where women are sexually subservient to men. The show has become a hit with the Resistance crowd on the left, many of whom think the world of *Handmaid's Tale* — adapted for TV and based on the best-selling novel by Margaret Atwood — is comparable to Trump's America.

During the Super Bowl, *Handmaid's Tale* ran an advertisement that used Ronald Reagan's famous "Morning in America" speech to paint a dystopian picture of America.

"HAIL SATAN!" PRO-ABORTION FANS

Bill Donohue comments on pro-abortion supporters in Texas:

While pro-life protesters were singing "Amazing Grace" yesterday in Austin, pro-abortion fans were screaming "Hail Satan!" (A video of this scene is available on TheBlaze.)

It would be unfair to say that all pro-abortion supporters would support this obscenity, and indeed most would not. Among hard-core activists, though, there are no doubt more than just a few who feel comfortable with invoking Satan's name in behalf of their cause. Here's why I say this.

There are writers and activists who support more than abortion rig[...] positive good. For example, the book by women's studies professo[...] *Abortion: A Positive Decision*, boasts how abortion liberates women. [...] *is a Blessing*, by militant atheist Anne Nicol Gaylor, sees abortion [...] does French author Ginette Paris: her book, *The Sacrament of Abor[...]* where she is coming from.

Catholics reach out to young pregnant women who have made the [...] indeed the Catholic Church has a program, "Project Rachel," that [...] ways. Moreover, when someone in the pro-life community acts in ar[...] quickly condemned. By contrast, there are pro-abortion fanati[...] inspiration from Satanic forces. Worse, many of those in the pro-abo[...] quite content to stay silent about such offenses.

Perhaps the time has come for a mass exorcism.

Pro-abortion fans demonstrate at the Texas Capitol. They repeatedly chanted, "Hail Satan!"

The Satanic Temple unveils its statue of Baphomet, a winged-goat creature, at a rally for the First Amendment in Little Rock, Ark., on Aug. 16, 2018. The Satanic Temple wants to install the statue on Capitol grounds as a symbol for religious freedom after a monument of the biblical Ten Commandments was installed in 2017. Photo courtesy of Magnolia Pictures

(RNS) — The Almighty may not think the Satanic Temple is a church.

But the taxman has given it the thumbs-up.

The Satanic Temple, which is featured in a documentary called "Hail Satan?," announced this week that the IRS now recognizes it as a church.

That recognition means the group can now get the same benefits as religious organizations — including tax exemption and protection from discrimination.

In a statement, Lucien Greaves, founder of the media-savvy group, said that "accepting religious tax-exemption — rather than renouncing it in protest — can help us to better assert our claims to equal access and exemption while laying to rest any suspicion that we don't meet the qualifications of a true religious organization."

"Satanism is here to stay," he added.

WORLD

6-Year-Old Boy Reportedly Tossed From 10th-Floor Building

Photo by Dan Kitwood/Getty Images

LEXI LONAS
CONTRIBUTOR

August 05, 2019
11:58 AM ET

A six year old boy is in stable condition after a teenager allegedly threw him off the tenth-floor viewing platform at London's Tate Modern gallery Sunday afternoon.

The boy landed on the fifth-floor roof and was airlifted to a hospital where he is now in critical, but stable condition. The 17-year old teenager who allegedly threw the boy off the roof has been arrested for attempted murder, according to the Associated Press.

Nancy Barnfield, the boy's mother, was at the gallery with her two sons. An admin worker said he heard Barnfield scream "my son, my son" and that she sounded terrified, The Telegraph reported.

A young boy and his mother were on the observation deck of the museum when a 17-year-old teenager, unknown to them, came up, grabbed the boy and threw him off the 10th floor viewing platform. The boy lived but was in critical condition at a hospital. Shocked observers said the teenager who assaulted the boy was calm and showed no emotion.

It Begins: "Death Camps to All Trump Supporters" Fliers Posted in New York

f 5.4K Share   299 Tweet   E

by Jim Hoft   August 7, 2019   605 Comments

New York – Fliers were posted on Tuesday calling for "Death Camps to all Trump Supporters."

New York is increasingly intolerant of conservative beliefs.

PJ MEDIA

🖬 337k 🐦 62.9k 🔲 📷   NEWSLE

COLUMNISTS NEWSLE

NEWS & POLITICS   TRENDING   HOMELAND SECURITY   FAITH   LIFESTYLE

ROGER L. SIMON

From El Paso to Antifa to LA: America the Insane

BY ROGER L. SIMON AUGUST 4, 2019   💬 814 COMMENTS

(Edvard Munch, 1893, The Scream, National Gallery of Norway)

Predictably, Beto O'Rourke fairly sprinted down to his hometown of El Paso to blame Donald Trump for the city's mass murders in the hope of reigniting the Texan's failing presidential campaign. But if you read the gunman's manifesto, you would find the murderer as much in agreement, possibly more so, with Elizabeth Warren and O'Rourke himself than with Trump. The shooter wants universal healthcare and a guaranteed income. He also wants to kill Mexicans and to partition the country into equal race-based sections, a kind of identity politics taken to the nth power, not that any of this matters. The man is clearly insane, as was the now-deceased Dayton killer who was reportedly a Democrat and a Satanist, planning on voting for Warren, as well as, of course, being mentally ill. ("I want socialism, and I'll [sic] not wait for the idiots to finally come round to understanding," the Dayton shooter tweeted.)

This is obviously not politics in any rational sense, although we are hearing endless political statements from pols anxious to exploit the tragedy. *It's about craziness.* An epidemic is sweeping the country and has been for some time. Mass shootings are only one manifestation, although arguably the most horrible and extreme one.

It may not immediately seem to be so, but the expanding homeless populations all over the streets of Los Angeles, San Francisco, and Seattle are another salient example. These people are hugely disturbed, unwilling to live in shelters, some quite well-equipped, that have been built for them. They prefer to live in tents more hospitable to their lifestyle that frequently involves drugs and to be left alone with their delusions while defecating on the sidewalks. Neighborhoods are being destroyed as a result.

And then there's Antifa. Is running around in masked costumes smashing windows and beating people in the name of fighting "fascism" an example of sanity or derangement? Obviously the latter. Antifa is yet another tragedy waiting to happen. Their mirror images, white supremacist groups, are similar manifestations of severe emotional disturbance with obvious violent implications.

All these people and groups are connected by their high level of psychological disturbance. Their number is small, even tiny, compared to the total population, but our population is approaching a giant 330 million. If only one-tenth of one percent of that number is seriously disturbed, that's 330,000 dangerous nut cases (excuse the non-clinical terminology) walking around in our country.

Because of the sclerotic politics that we all have been living with since we were born, most of the discussion this week will be focused on gun control. It will be largely symbolic and almost entirely irrelevant. Ban AR-15s or not, people who wish to wreak havoc will have no trouble getting the weapons to do it. We've already seen that in places like Chicago and Paris that have stringent gun laws, yet have seen catastrophic gun violence.

The real discussion should be about mental health, not weaponry, but the former is far more difficult to deal with. Indeed, it's almost overwhelming. Ex post facto, almost all these mass murderers are easily classified as mentally ill, but only rarely are they interdicted in advance. Law enforcement agencies, school administrators and other authorities have been reluctant to take action to prevent the disturbed from acting out for fear of repercussions to themselves or simply out of lassitude. This is not only true for the potential shooters, but it also helps explain why nothing has been done about the tent cities turning our most beautiful cities into Third World cesspits. Or the government in Portland allowing Antifa to run rampant. No one wants to be an adult anymore.

We're going to have to learn unless we want these events to be the new normal — or rather continue to be the new normal.

This commentator discusses the explosion of violence across America by lone serial killers as well as the socialist terror group, Antifa. He say that the population is showing extreme signs of "insanity."

Fellowship Of The Minds
"The greatest charity one can do to another is to lead him to the truth." -St. Thomas Aquinas

Woman who provided 65,000 abortions calls killing of unborn a "sacrament" and a "blessing"

Posted on December 28, 2014 by Dr. Eowyn | Leave a comment

Patricia Baird-Windle

On August 29, 1999, *Florida Today's* editorial page editor Pam Platt interviewed an abortion provider in Florida named Patricia Baird-Windle, 64, on the occasion of her retirement after 23 years and 65,000 legal abortions as the owner of the **Aware Woman Center for Choice** abortion clinics in Melbourne, Port St. Lucie and West Palm Beach, FL.

In its article, *Florida Today* extolled the baby-killer as "one of the stalwarts on the front lines of the abortion wars."

Here are excerpts of what Baird-Windle said in the interview (via Forerunner.com):

> "I now consider abortion to be a major blessing, and to be a sacrament in the hands of women."
>
> "Now that there's no longer the need for children to work farms and in factories, we should recognize that women should always have the absolute right to say when and where and how they are going to be a parent."
>
> "This [abortion] is perhaps the biggest social change ever in women's lives. Many personality types don't like change at all, and this particular change, one that clearly places the power in the woman's hands, is just desperately upsetting to the authoritarian male and some females."
>
> [Asked whether she sees herself as what opponents of abortion call her, a baby-killer who fosters a culture of death and who provides abortion for money, Baird-Windle said] "Not for one New York minute. (Laughs.) I knew better. A. I know how stupid they are. B. I know how venal they are."
>
> [Asked whether she ever thinks providing abortion is wrong or immoral, and how she sleeps at night, Baird-Windle said] "If you're referring 'sleep at night' to any form of guilt, **there is no form of guilt** when you know what you're doing is giving a woman power over her life, and when she's doing the right thing."

Fellowship Of The Minds
"The greatest charity one can do to another is to lead him to the truth." -St. Thomas Aquinas

American Psychological Association to promote adultery, swinging & orgies

Posted on July 11, 2019 by Dr. Eowyn | 25 Comments

Psychology is already at best a soft, if not outright pseudo, science.

Now the **American Psychological Association (APA)** is venturing into the non-scientific, non-empirical domain of morality by giving their approval to adulterers, swingers, and orgiasts.

In 1985, "a group of pioneering LGB psychologists and their allies" at the APA founded Division 44, the Society for the Psychological Study of Lesbian and Gay Issues, for an explicitly nonscientific, political reason. Div. 44's mission states:

> Div. 44 (SPSOGD) is committed to advancing social justice in all its activities. The Society celebrates the diversity of lesbian, gay, bisexual, transgender and gender nonconforming and queer people....

Div. 44 has over 1,500 members, and "represents" all 50 states, the District of Columbia, and 11 foreign countries "on every inhabited continent."

The latest Div. 44 initiative is the Consensual Non-Monogramy Task Force, the goal of which is to "promote awareness and inclusivity about consensual non-monogamy and diverse expressions of intimate relationships. These include but are not limited to: people who practice polyamory, open relationships, swinging, relationship anarchy and other types of ethical, non-monogamous relationships."

The AMA task force's justification for its promotion of open marriages, orgies ("polyamory": "the practice of having sexual or romantic relationships with two or more people at the same time"), swinging, and "relationship anarchy" (whatever that is) is that everyone should have the "liberty" to find "love and/or sexual intimacy" without "social and medical stigmatization".

This news item reported that the American Psychological Association not only celebrated the LGBT lifestyle, the large group of psychological professionals endorsed "adultery, swinging, orgies" and similar activities by individuals. Can we depend on such unscientific people—supposedly professionals—to diagnose dangerous psychopaths and to advise us about the depths of their outrageous behavior? (Note: The polluted attitudes of today's psychologists and their therapeutic personnel is one of the main reasons that I authored this book.)

SWEDISH SCIENTIST PROPOSES CANNIBALISM TO FIGHT CLIMATE CHANGE

f 178,158	✉ EMAIL	🔴 SHARE	🐦 TWEET

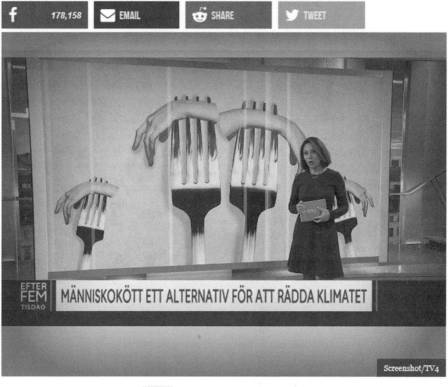

EFTER FEM TISDAG — MÄNNISKOKÖTT ETT ALTERNATIV FÖR ATT RÄDDA KLIMATET

Screenshot/TV4

by CHRIS TOMLINSON | 6 Sep 2019 | 63,946

▶   🎧 LISTEN TO STORY   2:08

Swedish behavioural scientist Magnus Söderlund has suggested that eating other people after they die could be a means of combatting climate change.

The scientist mentioned the possibility of cannibalism during a broadcast on Swedish television channel TV4 this week about a fair in Stockholm regarding "food of the future".

Söderlund is set to hold seminars at the event, entitled "Gastro Summit — about the future of food" where he intends to discuss the possibility of eating people in the name of cutting down greenhouse emissions.

Regardless of the likely immense resistance to the idea of eating people, Söderlund said it was important to examine different options in the name of sustainability.

Söderlund is not alone in his call to reject the taboo of cannibalism. Last year, noted atheist and evolutionary scientist Richard Dawkins advocated for lab-grown meat and suggested it may be used to "overcome our taboo against cannibalism".

B BREITBART

UNION THEOLOGICAL SEMINARY HOLDS 'CONFESSION TO PLANTS' IN CHAPEL CEREMONY

| f 709 | ✉ EMAIL | 👽 SHARE | 🐦 TWEET |

Facebook/Union Seminary

by THOMAS D. WILLIAMS, PH.D. | 18 Sep 2019 | 752

▶ 🎧 LISTEN TO STORY 2:45

New York's non-denominational Union Theological Seminary (UTS) held a ceremony Tuesday where members of the community placed plants in the center of the chapel and confessed their sins to them.

"Today in chapel, we confessed to plants," UTS tweeted, together with a picture of the ritual. "Together, we held our grief, joy, regret, hope, guilt and sorrow in prayer; offering them to the beings who sustain us but whose gift we too often fail to honor."

On Wednesday, after receiving a fair amount of derisive feedback, the seminary sent out a flurry of tweets defending its actions.

"When Robin Wall Kimmerer spoke at Union last year, she concluded her lecture by tasking us—and all faith communities—to develop new liturgies by which to mourn, grieve, heal and change in response to our climate emergency," one UTS tweet said. "We couldn't be prouder to participate in this work."

"So, if you're poking fun, we'd ask only that you also spend a couple moments asking: Do I treat plants and animals as divinely created beings?" another tweet proposed in its ecological examination of conscience. "What harm do I cause without thinking? How can I enter into new relationship with the natural world?"

Chapter Eleven

A Bloody Legacy: Psychopaths Throughout History

"To choose one's victims, to prepare one's plan minutely, to slake an implacable vengeance, and then to go to bed… There is nothing sweeter in the world."

—Joseph Stalin

Throughout history, mankind has been tormented and bedeviled by psychopaths who were able to stir up hatred and evil in multitudes of followers.

In Mexico, Central and South America, the monstrously barbaric Aztecs, Olmecs, Incas, and Mayans kidnapped and massacred tens of thousands of sacrificed victims. Later, history reveals that the ancient Jews, led by psychopaths, engaged in heinous and deadly warfare with the peoples around them. The noted historian Edward Gibbon, in his classic book, *History of the Decline and Fall of the Roman Empire* wrote of their many crimes:

"From the reign of Nero to that of Antonius Pius (0-160 CE), the Jews discovered a fierce impatience of the dominion of Rome, which repeatedly broke out in the most furious massacres and insurrections. Humanity is shocked at the recital of the horrid cruelties which they committed in the cities of Egypt, of Cyprus, and of Cyrene, where they dwelt in treacherous friendship with the unsuspecting natives… In Cyrene they massacred 220,000 Greeks; in Cyprus 240,000; in Egypt a very great multitude. Many of these victims were 'sawed asunder,' according to a precedent in which David had given the sanction of his example. The victorious Jews devoured the flesh, licked the blood, and twisted the entrails like a girdle around their bodies" (Vol. 2 Chap. XVI, part I).

For many years now I have diligently and meticulously studied and researched the role of psychopaths in history, taking careful note of their origins, doctrines and objectives. In all my investigations, one clear fact has stood out. The psychopaths are the most bloodthirsty group of savages that have ever walked the earth. Far from being a cultured, refined, and sophisticated elite, the psychopaths have demonstrated over and over again their pagan instincts and their obsessive and remarkable bloodlust.

The ongoing revolutions of the psychopaths—from the days of Spain's Loyola and the Alumbrados to Voltaire and Robespierre of the French Revolution, and on to Lenin and Trotsky of Bolshevik Soviet infamy and Mao and Pol Pot of Asian barbarism, a trail of terror and blood has been the identifying sign of these "enlightened" Luciferian man-gods.

Age of Terror

The prime legacy of the psychopaths these past 3,000 years has been their Revolutions of Blood. It is significant that historians have branded the period of the French Revolution the *Age of Terror*. Likewise, chroniclers of Leninism in Soviet Russia call the years 1917-1923 the time of the *Red Terror*.

In France, in 1798, the Freemason Voltaire privately told his Jacobin Illuminati co-conspirators, *"Our real object is to crush the wretch."* The "wretch" to whom Voltaire referred was Jesus Christ. And so, a small band of determined plotters, organized by Adam Weishaupt, a Jesuit professor who has been called "a human devil," set out to destroy all organized religion, murder every minister and priest, dismantle civilization, and return mankind to a primitive, savage state.

In his classic textbook, *Memoirs Illustrating the History of Jacobinism*, describing the Illuminist plot in France, Abbe Barruel affirms that "The grand object of this conspiracy was to overturn every altar where Christ was adored." Theirs, Barruel wrote, was an "unrelenting hatred for Christ and kings." Obviously, this hatred exists to this very day.

Liberty, Equality, Fraternity

The rallying cry and motto of the Illuminati in France was, *"Liberty, Equality, Fraternity!"* Seemingly, worthy goals. But in reality, the actual meaning and operation of these three terms were diabolical.

The word *"Liberty,"* to psychopaths means liberty of man from God, the liberty of man to do as he wants, when he wants, free of the shackles of the Christian religion. Rebellion and anarchy are to be used to achieve such liberty.

"Equality," meanwhile, implies that all authority is to be smashed and that no man should own more goods than his fellows. Man would have little or no property to tie him down, no family or children, no cities, no government. Instead, rewilded man would live pure in nature in a savage and primitive, yet exalted, state.

"Fraternity" means that all men are to be brothers, the artificial strictures of national borders, religions, and races, etc. obliterated.

To attain these deceptive goals of Liberty, Equality, Fraternity, a Masonic physician, Dr. Guillotine, invented a bloody, head-chopping blade machine, and heads began to roll. The King and the Queen were just two of thousands executed. Next, perceiving the guillotine as too cumbersome and slow—only one person at a time was beheaded—other killing methods were employed.

Christians in towns and cities across France who refused to renounce Christ were bound hand and foot and loaded onto boats. The boats were pushed into deep waters. Riflemen would then shoot holes in the boats. Plaintive screams and cries were heard

France's King
Louis XVI was
beheaded by
revolutionaries.

Robespierre

as the vessels sank and helpless, bound Christians drowned.

Protestant ministers and Catholic priests alike had their eyes gouged out. Many were shot, others bayoneted, still others stomped to death or killed with the sword. Crazed rioters tore many to pieces. Some who renounced Christ was spared after being humiliated.

Inside churches, revolutionary mobs shattered stain glass windows, defecated on and destroyed pews, and threw down crosses and urinated on them. In some churches, naked women paraded inside as "Lady Liberty," proceeded to the altar where they were adored and pawed at by drunken revelers shouting obscenities at God. Pornographic art was displayed in galleries and in homes.

Across France, over three million people perished—many of whom were small merchants and shop owners, simple farmers, and God-fearing elderly persons. In some cases, entire towns were razed and destroyed.

Finally, the executors became the executed. Robespierre, chief of the psychopathic butchers, was, in turn, himself dragged to the gallows and his head lopped off. It was the bloodthirsty feasting upon the bloodthirsty. Terror begetting terror.

When the Terror finally exhausted itself, the fake messiah, Napoleon, appeared on the scene. Many more died in the wars and famine that ensued after the crowning of the little Corsican dictator.

Of Barbarians and Devils

It was, however, in Russia and the Soviet republics that the psychopaths brought bloody terror to its ultimate peak in demonic perfection. As Donn de Grand Pré, in his sensational book, *Barbarians Inside the Gates*, reveals, the French and the Bolshevik (Communist) revolutions were funded, incited and supervised by satanic psychopaths. Marx, whose literary works inspired the Russian Revolution and Terror, was a satanist. Lenin, who led the bloody revolution in Russia, was definitely a satanic psychopath. Trotsky, Lenin's deputy and co-barbarian, was also a vicious barbarian. His demented brain showed psychopathic tendencies.

Killing Rabbits, Executing People

In *Under the Sign of the Scorpion*, a stunning book published in Sweden and written by Juri Lina, the author uses freshly unearthed historical archives from Russia to explain the Red Terror. Lina notes that Lenin's own wife, Nadezhda Krupskaya, in her *Memoirs* (1932), describes how Lenin once rowed a boat out to a little island in the Yenisei River where many rabbits had migrated during the winter. For his own sick pleasure, the cruel Lenin clubbed so many rabbits to death with the butt of his rifle that the boat sank under the weight of all the dead bodies. Lenin became drunk with glee at the awful sight.

As dictator, Lenin adopted the merciless terror methods of France's psychopathic chief, Robespierre. To help in the killing, Lenin mobilized 1,400,000 associates, putting many to work for the Cheka secret police. Lenin ordered the Cheka to *"execute weapons owners!"* They were also to kill as many students as possible, including every youth seen wearing a school cap.

Concentration camps were set up from which victims never emerged. Barges were used to drown people. Eyes of churchmen were poked out, tongues cut off, hands sawn off, heads drilled with dental tools—while screaming victims were still alive. Those nearby were forced to cut off the scalp and skull of victims and eat their brains, then, they, too, were executed. Whole families were arrested, mothers brutally raped and killed with children and fathers watching. Then all were grotesquely tortured and killed. The Volga and other rivers ran red with blood.

Churches almost everywhere were razed and bulldozed to ruins or converted to warehouses. A few were spared so the Communists could claim freedom of religion was being honored.

Put More Force Into the Terror

Lenin and Trotsky were, nevertheless, never satisfied. "Put more force into the terror," Lenin demanded. The Russian newspaper *Yevreyskaya Tribuna* (August 24, 1922), stated that Lenin had asked underlings if they were satisfied with the particularly cruel executions meted out to the Christian clergy and followers.

Lina shows in his book how Lenin saw his Bolshevik Revolution as the mirror image of the French Revolution. Indeed, he was correct—both were products of horrific skullduggery. The French revolutionists wanted a One World Order with God dethroned. So did Lenin's Communist revolutionaries.

In August 1923, with syphilis ravaging his mind, an ailing Vladimir Lenin sat on his balcony at Christmas and howled at the full moon like a wolf. A few weeks later, he was dead. But the Red Terror had only begun. Lenin's bloody successor, Joseph Stalin, was at his bedside ready to assume Lenin's mantle as chief executioner. From 1923 to his own death in the 50s, Stalin saw to it that tens of millions more were purged, arrested, locked away in psychiatric

Vladimir Lenin, Illuminist and bloodthirsty patron of Communist Revolution, with his sister and doctor in August 1923. By this time, Lenin's mind was ravaged by syphilis and he was a raving maniac. Note the strange look in his eyes. Communist adorers in Russia built Lenin's mausoleum using the Babylonian temple in Pergamon (*Revelation*—"the seat where Satan dwells") as a prototype.

After Lenin's death, yet another psychopath, Joseph Stalin, assumed power in Soviet Russia. Under his direction, more than 50 million people were unmercifully slaughtered.

Stalin, as a young man, was a train and bank robber and a ruffian who did not hesitate to kill.

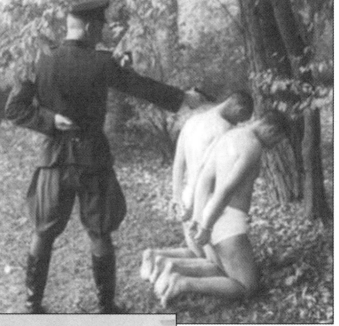

(Above) During World War II, many Polish prisoners of war were executed by Stalin's brutal and thuggish army.

Millions of innocent civilians were killed by Lenin and Stalin.

hospitals and gulags, and tortured in KGB chambers of horror.

The psychopaths who operated freely in the Soviet Empire intended that the whole world would be changed to meet their psychopathic needs. *Pravda*, the Soviet newspaper, on September 8, 1928, asserted, "Our program is an open war declaration for life and death against the entire world."

Pol Pot and His Genocide in Cambodia

"We were not allowed to cry or show any grief when they took away our loved ones. A man would be killed if he lost an ox he was assigned to tend. A woman would be killed if she were too tired and exhausted to work. Human life was not even worth a bullet. They clubbed the backs of our necks and pushed us down to smother us and let us die in a deep hole with hundreds of other bodies."

These are the sorrowful words of Teeda Mam, a victim and survivor of a Cambodian death camp, as reported in Dith Pran's book, *Children of Cambodia's Killing Fields*.

In the 1970s, the Communist regime in Cambodia methodically and without the smallest tinge of human sympathy or compassion saw to the abduction, torture, incarceration and death of up to three and a half million of its own citizens. Men, women, and children suffered unfathomable cruelty and deprivation. Numerous torture centers were set up and prisoners were duly numbered and "processed." Beatings, starvation, rapes, and the most savage tortures were inflicted. It was as if all

Pol Pot, psychopath who carried out the horrible genocide in Cambodia. He was quoted as saying, "Better to kill a friend by mistake than to spare an enemy."

the hounds and beasts of hell were unleashed in one place at the same time.

Amazingly, until this time, the Cambodians had gained a reputation as being a gentle people occupying a land of smiles: friendly, humble city dwellers and peasants eager to demonstrate kind acts. Almost in a moment, many of these same "good" people were inspired to commit repugnant genocidal crimes of terrible dimensions.

The Communists, called the *Khmer Rouge*, were led by a terrorist named Pol Pot. Pot was educated in France, where he studied socialism and the tactics of Karl Marx and his Red Chinese hero, Mao Tse Tung. He theorized that Cambodia had to be "cleansed and purified." He ordered all cities to shut down and prescribed death to every person who had so much as finished high school. His goal was to start fresh, to obtain pure thinking.

Pol Pot turned out to be a psychopath of the first order. A monster without parallel. Lenin, Hitler, Stalin, and Mao Tse Tung were pikers compared to him. But in the West, in Europe, and in the United States, Pol Pot was greatly admired and even quoted by Marxists and socialists.

If in the future, a Communist or socialist regime led by psychopaths takes power, such a regime will undoubtedly receive enthusiastic support. Check out the photos and news clippings in my photographic section, *Crazy Times*, and you will gain a quick understanding of this psychopathy currently flowing across the United States.

At their trials for genocide in 2011, the Communist butchers who had slaughtered millions under the Khmer Rouge regime in Cambodia denied their crimes. Nuon Chea, the number two man in the Communist government, insisted that the Communists were "good people." His henchmen, Khieu Samphan and Ieng Sary, said they bore no responsibility for the atrocities.

News | Opinion | Sport | Culture

World ▶ Europe US Americas Asia Australia Middle East Africa Inequality Cities G

Khmer Rouge were not bad people, former leader tells court

Nuon Chea denies responsibility for deaths of 1.7 million people in Cambodia during the 1970s at UN-backed tribunal

▲ The Khmer Rouge number two, Nuon Chea, at the UN-backed hearing in Cambodia. Photograph: Reuters

A former leader of Cambodia's brutal Khmer Rouge regime has told a court he and his comrades were not "bad people", denying responsibility for the deaths of 1.7 million people during their 1970s rule and blaming Vietnam for any atrocities.

Nuon Chea's defiant statements came as a UN-backed tribunal began questioning him and two other Khmer Rouge leaders in court for the first time.

The long-awaited trial began late last month with opening statements, and this week the court is expected to focus on charges involving the forced movement of people and crimes against humanity. After the Khmer Rouge captured Phnom Penh on 17 April 1975, they began moving an estimated 1 million people, including hospital patients, from the capital into the countryside in an effort to create a communist agrarian utopia.

After a court clerk read a background of the Khmer Rouge and the three defendants, Nuon Chea defended the notoriously brutal former movement, in which he was the number two leader behind the late Pol Pot. "I don't want the next generation to misunderstand history. I don't want them to believe the Khmer Rouge are bad people, are criminal," Nuon Chea said. "Nothing is true about that."

The 85-year-old communist movement's one-time chief ideologist said no Cambodian was responsible for atrocities during the Khmer Rouge's 1975-1979 reign, reiterating a claim that neighbouring Vietnam instead

The bones of Pol Pot's victims are stacked like cordwood.

A painting of dead bodies, neatly placed in rows in a Cambodian prison.

Two victims of the Khmer Rouge. Millions perished.

The Cambodian Communist soldiers load a wheel cart with bodies of people just slain.

Chapter Twelve

Satanism, Sex Crimes, and Psychopathy in America

"But whoso shall offend one of these little ones which believe in me, it were better for him that a millstone were hanged about his neck, and that he were drowned in the depth of the sea."
— The words of Jesus; *Matthew 18:6*

Imagine an elite group of evil child molesters meeting privately in an undisclosed location. Imagine, too, these wicked sexual predators making plans to conduct grotesque, real-life experiments on innocent little boys and girls. In these experiments, the children will be systematically raped, sodomized, and physically violated. Detailed records will be kept of the children's reactions so that pedophiles worldwide can "enjoy" seeing the results.

Satanic Doctor to Conduct Experiment

Next, imagine this elite group deciding that these horrendous sexual experiments are to be supervised by a well-known professor, or "doctor," of zoology. The chosen doctor happens to be an admirer of the infamous British satanist, Aleister Crowley (the Beast), and is himself a pedophile and homosexual. He will be given millions of dollars to set up a sexual laboratory and institute at a public university somewhere in Middle America.

After this doctor's depraved team completes its abominable research, the mass media will be employed. The nation's newspapers, television, and radio, along with educational organizations, will join in congratulating the pedophile research doctor on a job well done. His name as a great thinker and scientist will go up in lights. The whole world shall sing his praises and be joyful for what this man has done to these little children, all in the name of science.

The Work is Begun and is Successful

And so it is that the doctor of zoology and his helpers go about their grim business of sexual molestation. Thousands of children are thrown into beds. Pedophile molesters described as "research associates" repugnantly and with wicked abandon ravage their cringing, young bodies. Some infants molested are only five months of age. The abused children are counted as statistics and labeled as "scientific subjects."

All goes according to plan. The satanist doctor's name becomes a household word. Educators toast his brilliance. Commendatory books are published examining his work and touting his findings. Clergymen and readers of mass circulation magazines — including family-oriented publications — agree with his conclusions and change their attitudes and behaviors accordingly.

No one seems upset. No one is alarmed. Yet, thousands of children are systematically tortured and raped. The majority of people rejoice that a stunning sexual revolution has taken place. Somehow, though, the world will never again be the same. Never.

A Horror Movie... or Real?

Could what I have just described be the makings of a raw and explicit horror movie? Or could it be real? Did these monstrously sordid events and acts actually take place, and in America no less, home of the brave and the free?

In fact, the scenes I have described are real. This vile plot and activity did take place — and not in Nazi Germany either. Not in Soviet Russia, not in Asia or in South America. These things happened in America in the lifetime of most of us. Furthermore, I believe they are still happening today as you read this. Hundreds, even thousands of little boys and girls are being offered upon the altar of pedophile sex magick. They are being abused regularly and often, and the authorities know about it and are doing nothing to prevent these filthy and ungodly crimes from occurring.

Albert Kinsey, Psychopath Researcher and Pedophile

In her mind-absorbing book, *Kinsey: Crimes and Consequences — The Red Queen and the Grand Scheme*, Dr. Judith Reisman explodes the strange and malevolent myth of Albert Kinsey, the world-acclaimed satanic doctor responsible for this outrageous

criminal atrocity. It was Kinsey who burst on the scene in the early 50s with his widely admired but shocking *The Kinsey Report*. The findings in this report were based on Kinsey's book, *Sexual Behavior in the Adult Male*. In it, the now-famous Indiana University sex researcher claimed that homosexuality — as well as almost any other deviant and perverted sexual activity — is natural and normal. Children, said Kinsey, are sexual from birth, even in the crib. Kids just a year or two old were claimed to want "positive" sex and said to enjoy pleasurable feelings from sexual activity.

As this staged photo illustrates, the Illuminati's public relations machine, with Rockefeller funding, created an image of Kinsey as a nice, caring, family-oriented researcher. In fact, he and his associates were part of an international ring of sadistic, pedophile child torturers and abusers.

Kinsey is shown here visiting satanic high priest Aleister Crowley's temple at Thelema, in Sicily, with occult porno film maker Kenneth Anger. This photograph was obviously posed to create deeply occult symbols and images.

Children Strapped Down and Abused

Reisman's astonishing book documents some of the fiendish ways in which Dr. Kinsey and his institute carried out much of their research. For example, children three to seven years in age were regularly strapped or held down while grotesque sexual acts were performed on them. Stopwatches were often used to time the children's physical response.

Judith Reisman appropriately asks: "Where were the police and law enforcement authorities when these disgraceful and outrageous criminal acts were being committed? Where is the outrage in the academic community and the mass media today? Why, seemingly, is no one disturbed or alarmed at these atrocities committed in the name of science?"

Adult Sex with Children Normal

Kinsey's research findings were that adults who used children for "sex outlets" were quite normal. One Kinsey research associate, who was reported to have had various forms of sexual activity with 800 children, was deemed by Kinsey to be a "refined gentleman" and a "scientific hero." Government funds were used to help compensate this serial child molester for his contributions to science!

From Kinsey's flawed research conclusions a new generation built an entire, new working theory of sexual freedom and license. Kinsey was described by the press and the academic world as the "Father of the Sexual Revolution." Author and novelist Gore Vidal, himself a notorious homosexual, candidly stated that Kinsey was "the most famous man in America, in the world."

Rockefeller, Kinsey, and the Grand Scheme

In her revealing book, Dr. Judith Reisman for the first time exposes Kinsey's satanist connections. She also unmasks the fact that it was the Rockefeller Foundation that gave the wicked Dr. Kinsey the money to conduct his sin-laden, genocidal, child soul-killing research.

At the heart of it all was a "Grand Scheme" by the late Kinsey and his associates to destroy the very building blocks of society. Their goal was to create a New Civilization. The decadent dream of the surviving conspirators remains. They are determined to create a nonjudgmental, anti-God world where homosexual pedophiles can treat children like slabs of meat at a neighborhood flesh market—plundering them in the name of "loving and caring for their needs."

Our Twisted and Sick Culture

Look around you, kind readers, and ask yourself: Why is our twisted and sick culture the way it is today? Why have even the youngest of our kids become sexual barbarians and menacing satanic warriors? Why is the MTV generation so devoid of a conscience? And what of their parents—the drug-crazed, sexually liberated, generation? This is an entire generation made into zombies by marijuana, cocaine, heavy metal music, and rap music. Between the mixed-up kids and their demented parents, America has become a dumbed-down psychopathic nation of unthinking and sexually weird immorals.

Can We Trust the "Professionals" to Properly Diagnose the Psychopaths?

This inability of psychiatrists and psychologists to properly diagnose psychopaths and to predict their awful behavior is clearly evidenced. Recently the news reported that a convict guilty of murdering his wife was sent to prison for a fifteen-year term. Released, he quickly went on to rape and murder a second woman. This time he spent 25 years behind bars, but was released by the parole board after the prison psychiatrist said that, at age 73, he was "too old" to commit further crimes. Within two days of being set free this callous and evil psychopath murdered yet another woman—a woman he had been stalking since the day he was released.

This demonstrates how entrusting our safety, even our very lives, with the so-called educated "experts" can prove to be a futile and dangerous exercise. Consider, if you will, how morally corrupt—in my opinion—are the members of the premier psychological professional group, the American Psychological Association (APA). In recent decades this organization, representing about 118,000 members, has continually lowered its standards to "accept" gay and transgender (LGBT) behavior. At one time, the APA's diagnosis for LGBT persons held their behavior to be a psychological disorder. No more. Why the dramatic change?

In an article, "Who were the APA Task Force Members?" (*Josephnicolosi.com*, June 11, 2015) analyzed the Task Force Members who in 2019 ruled that conversions of LGBT persons should not be attempted and that their debauched and irregular conduct was perfectly acceptable, Joseph Nicolosi reported that 6 out of 7 of the Task Force Members were themselves homosexual or lesbian. Nicolosi said that whereas only 1 to 2 percent of the U.S. population is gay, almost every individual who makes up the APA leadership is gay.

"Not only were the members gay, but all—including the one member who claimed not to be a gay—engaged in gay activism before their selection to the APA Task Force."

According to this actively gay Task Force, it is "unnatural" for LGBTs to live a religious life apart from the homosexual lifestyle. So the vast majority of psychologists who make-up the APA are not only promoting a dangerous and unwholesome lifestyle, they are also rejecting thousands of years of traditional religious experience.

Is it any wonder that the many reprobates of the APA cannot properly diagnose the unnatural, sick minds of the psychopaths who populate American Society?

LGBT (Lesbian, Gay, Bisexual, Transgender) people "enjoy" an outing while parading around nude. The American Psychological Association explains that these bizarre individuals are normal and not mentally sick. One wonders just how many LGBTs are *psychopaths*. Recently, a news item reported on two lesbians who adopted a young boy. The two lesbians did not like the boy's masculine gender and so they cruelly cut-off his penis. Both were arrested by the police.

A drag queen acts up at a LGBT gathering. Excited women donated cash to show their appreciation.

Free of an agenda (except that gay one)

dragstrip 66 | **This Queer Nightlife Legend Wants To Go On The Record To Inspire Weirdos Everywhere**

By Dan Tracer June 10, 2015 at 12:06pm

Gay parties are a dime a dozen in cities like Los Angeles, where you're just as likely to find corporate sponsors as you are gogo boys in designer underwear. Or to put it a bit less cynically, there are lots of *perfectly fine* events. And there's nothing wrong with a *perfectly fine* night out.

But every now and then something comes along that transcends the moment. Unfortunately for anyone who never attended Dragstrip 66, it's a *then* and not a *now*.

The legendary L.A. party got its start in 1993 and ran for an impressive 20 years, redefining what LGBT nightlife could offer inspiring offshoots in other cities — Squeezebox in New York and Trannyshack in San Francisco. Attendees wouldn't bat an eye to find themselves dancing next to Roseanne Barr, Drew Barrymore, Adam Lambert or Nina Hagen.

A "come as you are" inclusive atmosphere made this freak flag-flying event everything a party should be — a celebration of connection.

And the themes! "Florence Of Arabia," "Queen Acres," "Victor/Victoria's Secret," "Mi Navidad Loca" — the list goes on.

Now, some of the event's organizers and fans are working to raise money to produce **_Dragstrip 66: The Frockumentary (https://www.tubestart.com/projects/dragstrip-66-the-frockumentary/7996),_** co-directed by Phil Scanlon and Paul V. that will put all the magic in official record.

You can get a sense of it from some of the awesome imagery below, and if you want to find about the project, head here (https://www.tubestart.com/projects/dragstrip-66-the-frockumentary/7996):

Here is a report from queerty.com about a party that homosexual perverts called *Dragstrip66* that is thrown every year in Los Angeles.

Right: A homosexual celebrates his lifestyle at a Gay Pride parade.

Left: Gays, like these two, seem bent on publicly displaying their unconventional behavior.

Chapter Thirteen

The Politician: Most Dangerous Psychopath on Planet Earth

"At least half of the people who enter politics are undiagnosed psychopaths and the worst of the worst inevitably reach the higher levels of government (Congress, Senate, Governor, etc.)."
— Mike S. King
Author, *The Bad War*

We have surveyed the top professions where you and I find the most psychopaths. But as I have said, these manipulative, sick men and women are everywhere. They make our lives miserable, they are responsible for a majority of murders, assaults, robberies, burglaries, and embezzlements. They wantonly cheat or steal from bank accounts and take money from the unsuspecting. We, as taxpayers, pay again when these deviates are caught, tried, and put in prisons.

Thus, we see how dangerous and defective are the psychopaths—men and women who are the dregs of society. But the absolute worst of the psychopath is the political leader, cunning men and women who plot and scheme their way to the ultimate government positions, where they can do the most harm. From this high-up vantage point, they can manipulate the masses, rip off millions of dollars, and establish control over the lives of millions of innocent, hardworking, normal citizens.

A good friend of mine, Mike S. King, author of *The Bad War*, and other books on politics and psychology, is convinced that the greatest threat we face today is the "hard-core" political psychopath. He recently wrote:

"At least half of the people who enter politics are undiagnosed psychopaths. And the worst of the worst inevitably reach the higher levels of government (Congress, Senate, Governor, etc.), with at least 80% of the high climbers being hard-core psychopaths . . ."

To insure he was not misunderstood, King added:

"I'm talking about the type of individuals who should either be straight-jacketed and institutionalized in lunatic asylums, or locked away in heavy labor prisons."

These individuals, he said, are:

> "...true psychopaths, heartless, soulless, shameless devils who will smile in your face, charm you, and flatter you as he, or she, sticks the knife in your back."

> "This psychopath is often charismatic, likeable, and energetic. He lies effortlessly. He will draw anyone into his orbit that can serve to further his ambitions, or fuel his ego with narcissistic supply. He manipulates. He cheats. He sucks the lifeblood out of you and then, when you are no longer of any value to him, he will discard you like a used up lemon."

The political hard-core psychopath, King says, will play every emotional card in his manipulative arsenal to achieve his ends. He alternates between outbursts of anger and verbal abuse. He employs "flattery, fake empathy for others, false pity for himself, fake smiling or laughing, fake crying, fake humility, false charity and fake piety."

King is correct. Check out the faces of high climbing political psychopaths. Note how often Hillary Rodham Clinton distorts her facial gestures to simulate shock, pity, crying, happiness, anger and sadness. The same is true for Newt Gingrich, George W. Bush, Chuck Schumer, and Nancy Pelosi. Such gestures are extremely popular people skills which are really theatrical and contrived in nature.

This psychopath is an inferior character, yet because of his clever and melodramatic acting, his never-ending supply of lies and deceptive behavior, and especially due to his guiltless remorse, he rises to the top of the political ladder.

A Choice Between Two Evils

How often do you hear people complaining about their poor choices for political candidates? "It's a choice of the lesser of two evils," they will say. "In all the United States, with over 300 milllion people, how did the political parties choose these two inferior candidates?"

The political psychopath has a remarkable ability to persuade large masses of people to follow him, to believe in him. He uses their confidence to con them to accept his aggressive agenda, however dishonest and cruel.

Benjamin Walman, publisher of a journal on group psychology, writes, "Usually human cruelty increases when an aggressive sociopath (psychopath) gains an uncanny, almost hypnotic control over large numbers of people. History is full of chieftains, prophets, saviors, gurus, dictators, and other megalomanics who managed to obtain support and incited people to violence."

Devoid of conscience and lacking empathy, the political psychopath will lie to exploit. He feels no empathy for his victims and inwardly laughs at their misery. "Serves these stupid people right," he figures. He appeals to the citizenry for greater control of their lives. A police state will eventually ensue as he gains control. This police state will, of course, limit ownership of guns so that people cannot protect themselves. "It is for the good of the nation," he will emphasize.

Give the psychopath power over your life and believe me, you will live to regret it.

It is alarming to realize that hard-line political psychopaths rise high up in government and are so capable of deceiving the masses. But psychiatrists who have studied this field agree. Psychopaths may be imbeciles and morons. They may have a huge deficit in brain power, but their personalities, bravado, and their double minds facilitating them to lie and cheat equips them for high political office.

In the U.S. Congress, psychopathic congressmen will vote for legislation, warmly endorsing it; then, only a few weeks later, vote against the same bill, informing audiences that the legislation is totally unacceptable. You'll hear a senator explain, "I voted against it, before I voted for it." Such confusing behavior rattles some constituents, but leaves the politician able to bob and weave back and forth, fooling the non-observant masses.

Those masses, especially the young, are confused, but society and their psychopathic leaders cause them to think they are far superior to the older generation they have succeeded. A legion of ignorant teachers feeds the young silly and infantile ideas about communism and socialism being superior. Their teachers and college professors convince them that the music of yesterday's generation is retrograde junk—rap and satanic heavy metal are so much better. And they are taught that higher education must be free, that medical services must be free, that homosexuality is infinitely wonderful, and that all who do not agree must be rejected and scorned. Free speech is only speech that does not offend and the young must be listened to and heeded. They are so much more clever, and the elderly deserve to be humiliated and hurt.

All these ideas, of course, are products and imaginings of ideologized psychopaths. The deluded young join them in their insane quest for power and control. As *Fox* Television's Tucker Carlson recently wrote, "A mob of angry children is suddenly in charge of the country... They're drunk on power and looking for new people to hurt. Some day, we're going to look back on this moment with shame and horror."

America Now Populated With Political Psychopaths

Recent years have seen the population of psychopaths in America explode. As a result, America is now on the precipice of disaster. The psychopaths are stirring up anger by robbing working people, and the media are in on this heinous plot. Their lies fill our minds and divide the nation. Unity has been ruptured. Diversity is in and the nation has splintered into pieces as the psychopaths loudly proclaim that diversity is best. So, blacks and whites face off, economic differences multiply, and people take sides. The psychopaths revel in this manufactured diversity.

Jim Quinn, writing in *The Burning Platform* blog, described the current tragic situation exactly:

> "The staggering number of corrupt prostituted sociopaths (i.e., psychopaths) occupying positions of power within the government, corporations, media, military, churches, and academia has created a morally bankrupt empire... These sociopaths are not liberal or conservative. They are not Democrats or

Republicans. They are not beholden to a country or community. They care not for their fellow man. They don't care about future generations. They care about their own power, wealth and control over others. They have no conscience. They have no empathy. Right and wrong are meaningless in their unquenchable thirst for more. They will lie, steal, and kill to achieve their goal of controlling everything and everyone in this world. This precisely describes virtually every politician in Washington, D.C...."

Chapter Fourteen

Gallery of Political Psychopaths

In the following pages we review some of today's frontline political psychopaths. Note we profile Republicans *and* Democrats. Psychopaths oscillate from political ideology to ideology, joining forces with the group that will best benefit them. Never reliable, they shift from policy to policy, being incredibly flexible. These are brief looks at just a few psychopaths.

I could provide you with entire books on these politicians, but have time only for several characteristics.

My opinion is that these politicians are psychopaths. You may disagree with me. I recommend you read what I report here, then go and do your own research. You be the judge. Be sure to study the *Fifteen Characteristics of Psychopaths* in Chapter Four.

Former President Barack Obama—The "Me, Me, Me" Factor

Have you noticed that in his speeches Barack Obama incredibly uses the words "I, Me, and My" over and over? In a Chicago speech in 2014, Obama used the first person singular 199 times. President Abraham Lincoln's Second Inaugural Address used the first person singular one time. Following is the article by Coach Dave Daubenmire, "Is the Man in the White House Mentally Ill?"

> "I am not asking this with my tongue in my cheek. I am as serious as a judge. As I sit here and write, I am listening to Mr. Obama's press conference. Something is very wrong with this guy. He is either mentally ill or demon-possessed. Either choice is a possibility. But something is definitely wrong with him. He seems somehow inhuman.
>
> President Obama is a hollow man. He has no feelings. He feels no emotions. The human drama seems to have no outward effect on him. I watch him in his press conference. I watch his eyes as he responds to the media's questions. I believe he is a sick, dangerous man.
>
> I googled the word *sociopath*. A person with a psychopathic personality whose behavior is antisocial, often criminal, and who lacks a sense of moral

responsibility or social conscience.

Bingo. That's him. That's the guy living the life of President of the United States.

I went a bit further and googled *Characteristics of a Sociopath*. Read it for yourself. Permit me to summarize. You recognize his mental illness by these traits.

—An oversized ego

—Lying and showing manipulative behavior

—Incapable of showing empathy

—Lack of shame or remorse

—Staying eerily calm in dangerous situations

—Behaving irresponsibly or with extreme impulsivity

—Having few close friends

—Being charming, but only superficially

—Showing disregard for societal norms

—Have intense eyes

The man is either sick or non-human. He does not react like a normal human being. Consider this from the article:

> "Sociopaths can be very charismatic and friendly—because they know it will help them get what they want. They are expert con artists and always have a secret agenda."

> "People are so amazed when they find that someone is a sociopath because they're so amazingly effective at blending in. They're *masters of disguise.*

> "Their main tool to keep them from being discovered is the creation of an *outer personality.*

> "As a psychopath (or sociopath) is reported in a post for *Psychology Today*: 'You would like me if you met me. I have the kind of smile that is common among television show characters and rare in real life, perfect in its sparkly teeth, dimensions and ability to express pleasant invitation.'

"Sociopaths are dangerous. Some famous sociopaths in recent history include Charles Manson, Ted Bundy, Jeffrey Dahmer, and John Wayne Gacy.

"You laugh at me. You ridicule what I say because I compare him to serial killers. Go ahead. Laugh. He displays all of the characteristics of the above-mentioned goons. They were charismatic and likable.

"What kind of man plays golf after a young man's head is chopped off? What kind of man disappears for hours while some of his 'employees' are being killed overseas? What kind of man permits a deadly disease to be freely introduced into society? What kind of man believes his own lies?"

"President Obama is either sick or demon-possessed. Red flags are everywhere we look.

"Will anyone stop him? President Obama is a sick, dangerous man. I just thought someone needed to point that out."

Former President George W. Bush— "Please Don't Let Them Kill Me"

Christian author Frank Schaeffer writes this about George W. Bush:

"Who and what was George W. Bush? I believe he was our nation's first sociopath (e.g. psychopath) president.

"According to the textbook clinical definition, a sociopath is a person with a disregard for the rights of others. The sociopath is often a charming witty person who stage-manages his life to impress others while hiding his true character. His amicable attributes are cultivated to cover his major trait: the violation of the rights of others. A sociopath also shows a lack of regret for his actions…Sound familiar?

"It all started when George W. Bush presided over 152 executions while governor of Texas, more than any other modern-era American governor. It ended with the needless deaths of hundreds of thousands, including over 4,000 American war dead and over 30,000 wounded and counting, after George W. attacked Iraq, a country that had had nothing to do with the attack on America on 9/11.

"George didn't pardon one man or woman on his crowded death row.

Before running for the presidency he had already shown himself to be a crass, merciless bully, a man to whom killing came easily.

"Following Karla Faye Tucker's notorious execution in Bush's Texas, conservative commentator Tucker Carlson interviewed then Governor Bush about how the Board of Pardons had arrived at the determination on her clemency plea. Carlson reported that Bush, alluding to a televised interview which Karla Faye Tucker had given to Larry King, smirked and spoke mockingly about her. Here's a quote from Carlson's article (*Talk*, September 1999).

> "In the weeks before the execution, Bush says, 'A number of protesters came to Austin to demand clemency for Karla Faye Tucker.' 'Did you meet any of them?' I asked. Bush whips around and stares at me. 'No, I didn't meet with any of them,' he snaps."

> "I asked then-Governor Bush what Karla Faye Tucker requested of him in her letter.

> "'Please,' Bush whimpers, his lips pursed in mock desperation, 'don't kill me.' I must have looked shocked—ridiculing the pleas of a condemned prisoner who has since been executed seems odd and cruel—because he immediately stopped smirking."

"A man who mocked a woman he'd denied a pardon to was unfit to serve as president. A heartless bully is not who Americans want in the White House. He might rather have been a good candidate for psychological therapy. Why wasn't this story the subject of an editorial in every major newspaper when Bush ran for the presidency? This should have been the headline: "Bush the Merciless Mocked Condemned—Unfit to Serve."

"Maybe his crass sophomoric attitude toward suffering was why one reason

George the Merciless started a completely unnecessary war of choice so blithely and then prosecuted it so ineptly that many more American soldiers died and were maimed during the interminable occupation than during the war.

"George the Merciless hid his dead and wounded. No pictures of funerals or flag-draped coffins please! Let the 'little people' die without the dignity of having their passing recorded, mourned or protested by the nation. Out of sight, out of mind. Forget the soldiers. Just go shopping!

"Burying W's troops (literally and figuratively) was to be stage-managed along with everything else. But when his troops needed care, W the Merciless (who had sent them into the wrong war with the wrong equipment) fought to stop extra funding for educational and other veteran's benefits, saying it might tempt soldiers not to re-enlist because they would have better options.

"George the Merciless will go down in history as an inept bungler. But one hundred years from now, if America is still around, and if anyone cares, what he will be remembered for is just two things: the many needless deaths over which he presided, and his total lack of remorse.

"In other words, W. the Merciless will be remembered as America's foremost sociopath president, a man who left the White House with a smile on his face and the blood of hundreds of thousands on his hands. That is his legacy."

Hillary Rodham Clinton: Lesbian, Slut, Psychopath

Right Wing Watch, a project of the left-wing group, People for the American Way, is dedicated to monitoring and exposing the activities of the right-wing movement. On May 18th the group posted that conservative talk show host, Sandy Rios, reported that Hillary is a lesbian and "a deviant."

Rios is the governmental affairs director for the American Family Association. On May 25th, Rios asserted that President Obama's order that school bathrooms be transgender-inclusive would "mainstream pedophilia."

"Hillary Clinton embraces every sexual deviancy you can imagine," Rios said.

"There have been more than rumors swirling about her own sexual proclivities since before she became First Lady," Rios continued, "She's an advocate of gay marriage, and I mean a strong advocate. She's been endorsed by every radical homosexual activist group in the country, all the major ones, Human Rights Campaign and others, especially in New York. She gets that endorsement for a reason, you know, she gets it for a reason."

Above: Hillary and her alleged lover Huma Abedin.

Right: Sandy Rios, governmental affairs director for the American Family Association reported that Hillary Clinton is a lesbian and "a deviant."

Hillary Clinton staring at Christina Aguilera's breasts.

(Note by Texe Marrs: I first reported that Hillary is a lesbian in my bestselling book, *Big Sister is Watching You*, 1993).

According to a previous report by Sandy Rios, the proof of Hillary Clinton's lesbianism can be found in her relationship with Huma Abedin, her administrative assistant, and also is embedded in her video of her presidential announcement.

In yet another commentary on Clinton's alleged lesbianism, Rios says:

"Please keep in mind that Hillary Clinton was one of the first public officials to push this whole notion of embracing homosexuality. I would never forget my own personal shock in the late 90s when there was a women's conference in Beijing and Hillary Clinton was in charge and they brought in women from all over the world at this UN conference, and the emphasis for the American delegation under Hillary's tutelage was on lesbianism."

National Enquirer ran a story on Hillary and Huma with the headline "Hillary Hides Huma Amidst Lesbian Rumors." The story links to another *National Enquirer* story from March 3rd which claims that Hillary is panicked about the possibility of emails she exchanged with Huma being revealed in public. That article is titled "Hillary Clinton Lesbian Love Letters—Panic Over D.C. Investigation."

The story has myriad photos of Hillary and Huma and notes the former Secretary of State is "terrified of revelations about her secret lesbian lifestyle."

Another well-known conservative publication, the *Daily Caller*, quotes Sally Miller, a former Miss Arkansas who asserts she's a former girlfriend of Bill Clinton, saying that the former president told her Hillary had had lesbian relationships while an undergraduate at the all-women's college, Wellesley.

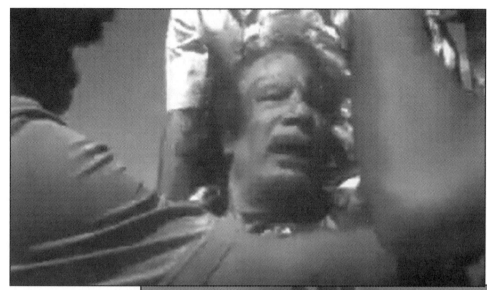

Libya's Gaddafi was horribly tortured by U.S. paid terrorists.

Psychopath Hillary Clinton is exuberant as she tells reporter of her being responsible for the murder of Muammar Gaddafi by U.S.A.-allied terrorists in Libya.

Hillary Clinton, Secretary of State, again happily celebrated the deaths of Arabs she claimed were terrorists.

As Secretary of State, a corrupt Hillary Clinton received billions of dollars from foreign countries who received "favors" in return.

Miller, who the *Daily Caller* says has released a tell-all memoir entitled *The Beauty Queen: Let No Deed Go Unpublished* of her and Bill Clinton's relationship is quoted as saying, "I take (Bill Clinton) at his word and he told me (Hillary) liked females more than men. She was the child of a more Progressive community."

Mr. Conservative, a conservative website, asserted in 2014 and 2015 that Hillary would face lesbian rumors if she ran for president. Fred Klein, on his website, asserted that Hillary was obsessed with lesbianism, but not in a normal way. Instead, she was much more interested in lesbianism as a political statement than as a sexual practice. Hillary talked about it a lot, read lesbian literature, and embraced it as a revolutionary concept.

In 2011 Hillary Clinton laughed about killing Libya's leader Muammar Gaddafi. "We came, we saw, he died," she joked when told of news reports of Gaddafi's death. Then she threw back her head and cackled loudly, like a loon.

***Hillary Clinton Sends Thank you Letter to "Slut" who is proud of her sexually transmitted disease* (Paul Joseph Watson, *Infowars*).**

Hillary Clinton sent a thank you letter to a woman who gained notoriety for celebrating the fact that she was a "slut" and had contracted herpes, a sexually transmitted disease.

Ella Dawson obtained brief internet fame earlier this year when she launched a campaign backed by the hashtag, "ShoutYourStatus" to encourage young women to embrace their STDs, arguing that there shouldn't be a social stigma surrounding the issue.

Hillary Clinton sent a thank you letter to a woman who gained notoriety for celebrating the fact that she was a "slut" and had contracted herpes, a sexually transmitted disease.

"I'm a slut, and I have herpes. I still am a person who deserves respect." Tweeted Dawson at the time.

Like all feminists who spout absolute stupidity and then claim victimhood status when they get any kind of blowback, Dawson instantly received a barrage of criticism before claiming she was the target of a harassment campaign.

She then wrote an essay whining about how the "sexist trolls" that comprise the 'Alt-Right' had subjected her to abuse.

The sum of the "abuse" was a *YouTube* video and it was pointed out that having genital warts because you're a "slut" isn't an accomplishment.

In her article, Dawson complains that as a result of this video, she received hundreds of messages from people calling her "insert the sexist slur of your choice here." In one example she cites, a *Twitter* user calls her a "whore."

This from the woman who calls herself a "slut" and says she is proud of it.

So she celebrates the fact she is a slut, but then cries about "harassment" when other people call her a whore, if that makes any sense (hint it doesn't).

Hillary Clinton appears to agree with Dawson that sleeping around is an achievement and sent Dawson a letter praising her for turning sexually transmitted diseases into a social justice cause.

"I am so grateful to you for not only speaking out against the stigma," Clinton wrote, "but for also taking a courageous stand against the ridiculous, but very real, barrage of hate you have received online."

Of course, in the real world, some things are stigmatized because discouraging them is the right thing to do. Herpes can damage the central nervous system and lead to other illnesses such as Alzheimer's disease. It's also contagious.

Being a slut isn't something to be proud of—it's a terrible lifestyle choice.

Dawson, already a vehement Hillary supporter, said she sobbed when she received and read Clinton's letter and that she resonated with Hillary's comments.

"It filled me with genuine, raw hope for the first time since I became an activist," she said.

Apparently, Dawson still thinks that encouraging other young women to become "sluts" and catch STDs is a form of activism.

Newt Gingrich: Terribly Wicked Man in Politics

Is he a Republican, a Democrat, or perhaps a Fascist or Communist? None of these! Newt is a psychopath.

Gingrich is clearly one of the most wicked men in politics. We start off by reminding readers that he was instrumental as House speaker in passing NAFTA. In fact, Gingrich has been called "Mr. NAFTA." Donald Trump says that NAFTA is the "Most deadly, job-killing trade bill" ever passed.

While Speaker of the House, Gingrich loved to be called a "New Ager." Gingrich has said that New Deal socialist Franklin D. Roosevelt is the "greatest President who ever served." Gingrich wrote the Foreword for the Tofflers' Marxist book, *Creating a New Civilization*, and personally gave every member of the House of Representatives a gift copy, so impressed was he with Tofflers' satanic, anti-American viewpoint.

What exactly do the Tofflers endorse in *Creating a New Civilization* that Gingrich fell for? I give actual quotes from the sick book below, but let me say here that it calls for "new family styles, a new economy…and altered political consciousness."

The book, *Creating a New Civilization*, also pushes for the end of outmoded

Newt Gingrich former Speaker of the U.S. House of Representatives, strongly endorsed the book, *Creating a New Civilization*, by Alvin and Heidi Toffler. That notorious book, in turn, parrots the scheme to destroy the Constitution of the United States and set up a Fascist World Order. Significantly, Newt Gingrich is a member of the CFR and also the World Future Society. As shown on one of their publications the logo of the World Future Society appears strikingly similar to a circular, 6-6-6 configuration.

"Nationalism" and for "more diverse religious systems."

"The Constitution needs to be reconsidered...the system must die," says the book.

And just what kind of "culture" does Mr. Gingrich want to see take hold in America? In my insightful, eye-opening book, *Circle of Intrigue*, I unmask the traitorous anti-American intentions of Gingrich and his associates in crime. "I have an enormous political ambition," Gingrich told *The Washington Post*. "I want to shift the entire planet and I'm doing it."

This planetary shift of Gingrich's takes a number of dangerous forms. It is, in fact, all part of the revolutionary socialist movement which Gingrich calls the "Third Wave." The Plan calls for nothing less than to radically change America into a fascist "paradise" with citizens stripped of constitutional rights. What is planned is a virtual high tech prison, an Orwellian Police State superintended by the self-appointed "Masters."

Gingrich has not been shy about presenting his "Third Wave" Plan. He flatly states that his goal is to end the old America forever. Insiders Alvin and Heidi Toffler enlisted the endorsement of Gingrich and the three set forth this Plan in the Tofflers' volume, *Creating a New Civilization*. Here are just a few more Third Wave principles espoused in the book by the Tofflers, with a Foreword by Gingrich.

> "The time has come for the next great step forward in American politics... to transition to what we call a 'Third Wave' information-age society...

> "A new civilization is emerging in our lives, and blind men everywhere are trying to suppress it. This new civilization brings with it new family styles, changed ways...a new economy, new political conflicts, and... altered consciousness... Humanity faces a quantum leap forward. This is the meaning of the Third Wave...

GALLERY OF POLITICAL PSYCHOPATHS

"Our argument is based on what we call the 'revolutionary premise'...The revolutionary premise liberates our intellect and will.

"Nationalism is...First Wave. The globalization of business and finance required by advancing. Third Wave economies routinely puncture the national 'sovereignty' the nationalists hold so dear...

"As economies are transformed by the Third Wave, they are compelled to surrender part of their sovereignty... Poets and intellectuals of Third Wave states sing the virtues of a 'borderless' world and 'planetary consciousness.'

"The Third Wave...demassifies culture, values, and morality... There are more diverse religious belief systems.

"The Constitution of the United States needs to be reconsidered and altered...to create a whole new structure of government... Building a Third Wave civilization on the wreckage of Second Wave institutions involves the design of new, more appropriate political structures... The system that served us so well must, in its turn, die and be replaced."

To say that these proposals mesh with the Plan and Great Work of the Satanists is a gross understatement. Gingrich and Toffler openly declare their goals: to smash Christianity, end American sovereignty, erase all international borders, wreck our entire existing civilization and kill off America's 200-plus year constitutional history forever. Gingrich is a Communist revolutionary who dares to state outright that he intends to destroy the United States and set up a totalitarian New World Order.

Kurt Nimmo, a patriotic columnist, states bluntly, "In no sense is Newt Gingrich a conservative or even a traditional Republican. He was a Fellow at neocon criminal organizations... Newt Gingrich has also attended Bohemian Grove where he rubbed elbows with occultists and male prostitutes...he is a demonstrated liar." (*Infowars. com*, April 23, 2010)

Yet amazingly, except for Nimmo and a few others, no-one has reported the atrocities of Newt Gingrich. The man continues to be lionized by the Republican Party. He is a frequent "talking head"—indeed, he is a paid contributor—for *Fox News* TV. Everywhere, the elite applaud his every move!

Gingrich revealed to Congress that he began working with the Tofflers in the early 1970s on a concept called "anticipatory democracy." He says, "For twenty years we (who's we?) have worked to develop a future-conscious politics and popular understanding that would make it easier for America to make the transition from the Second Wave civilization (the one the founders gave us)—which is clearly dying—to the emerging, but in many ways undefined, Third Wave civilization (Alvin Toffler's Utopia)."

According to *Science* magazine, Gingrich changed his view on climate change "from cautious skeptic in the late 1980s to believer in the late 2000s to skeptic again during the 2016 campaign."

Gingrich has married three times. In 1962, he married Jacqueline May Battley, his former high school geometry teacher, when he was 19 years old and she was 26.

Although Jackie has insisted that her relationship with Gingrich began when he was 16, Gingrich has denied such claims, asserting instead that he was already 18 at the time. Gingrich had several extramarital affairs during his first marriage.

In the spring of 1980, Gingrich filed for divorce from Jackie after beginning an affair with Marianne Ginther.

In 1984, Jackie Battley Gingrich told *The Washington Post* that the divorce was a "complete surprise" to her. According to Jackie, in September 1980, Gingrich and their children visited her while she was in the hospital recovering from surgery for cancer, and Gingrich wanted to discuss the terms of their divorce. Gingrich has disputed that account. Although Gingrich's presidential campaign staff continued to insist in 2011 that his wife requested the divorce, court documents obtained from Carroll County, Georgia, indicated that Jackie had asked a judge to block the process stating that although "she has adequate and ample grounds for divorce...she does not desire one at this time (and) does not admit that this marriage is irretrievably broken."

According to L.H. Carter, Gingrich's campaign treasurer, Gingrich said of his first wife: "She's not young enough or pretty enough to be his wife. And besides, she has cancer." Gingrich has denied saying it.

In 1981, six months after his divorce from his first wife was final, Gingrich wed Marianne Ginther. Marianne helped control their finances to get them out of debt. Gingrich's daughter, Kathy Lubbers, described the marriage as difficult.

In 1993, while still married to Marianne, Gingrich began an affair with House of Representatives staffer Callista Bisek, more than two decades his junior. Gingrich was having this affair even as he led the impeachment of Bill Clinton for perjury related to Clinton's own extramarital affair. Gingrich filed for divorce from Marianne a few months after she had been diagnosed with multiple sclerosis. On January 19, 2012, Marianne alleged in an interview on ABC's *Nightline* that she had declined to accept Gingrich's suggestion of an open marriage. Gingrich disputed the account.

In August 2000, Gingrich married Callista Bisek four months after his divorce from Marianne was finalized.

Though he relentlessly pushes military spending and talks like a bigtime hawk, Gingrich avoided the Vietnam War through a combination of student and family deferments. In the presidential debate on January 7, 2012, Gingrich claimed that "I never asked for a deferment, I was married with a child, it was never a question." That sounded like a pretty solid defense until Ron Paul pointed out that he had a wife and two children when he was drafted—and he went anyway.

Grandiose Notions

Newt has a grandiose attitude and self-importance that's hard to believe. Since he was in college, he has been telling people he needs to lead America so he can change history and save us all from disaster. No exaggeration—check out this 1995 *New Yorker* profile. Darryl Conner, a Gingrich friend who Newt has hired to train congressmen, remembers first working with him 40 years ago, when Newt was 28 years old. "It couldn't have been more than a few days before he was talking about what he needed to do to save Western civilization."

Frank Gregorsky, Newt's former chief of staff, said he once asked Newt to be more philosophically coherent, and Gingrich replied "Saving civilization is hard. You

POLITICS

Gingrich's Great-Man Complex, From Sci-Fi to History

CONOR FRIEDERSDORF DEC 9, 2011

Who's been influencing the former Speaker? Those with far-seeing efforts at transformation are valued most

Over at History News Network, Ray Smock, the historian at the House of Representatives until the 1994 Republican takeover, has a piece up on Newt Gingrich's affinity for Isaac Asimov's *Foundation Trilogy*. "Newt liked the idea of one man shaping the destiny of

have to be fluid." Newt asked Frank to read Isaac Asimov's *Foundation* sci-fi trilogy explaining, "I think of things in hundred-year increments, so I wanted you to read Asimov, because that conveys the course of civilization over five hundred years, because that is how I think."

House Banking Scandal: Newt Bounced 22 Checks

Remember the House Banking scandal, where so many congressmen wrote rubber checks on government money? Newt hopes you don't, because he bounced 22 himself, which almost cost him reelection in 1992. His vote for the secret House pay raise, and the chauffeur who drove him around Washington in a Lincoln Town Car, didn't help.

"Conservatives, Stop the Insanity: Newt Gingrich is Horrible"

That's the headline by Michael Brendan Dougherty from the *Business Insider*, November 10, 2011. The article read: "Wake Up! Newt cares about Newt! He has NEVER been a conservative. Newt is for amnesty. In a *CNN* June debate, he used the word *heartless* against those that would like to deport illegal aliens as REQUIRED BY LAW!"

In 2004, Newt and House Speaker, Democratic Nancy Pelosi, had photographs taken of both of them promoting a global warming agenda. This was the third time he changed his mind on climate change.

Gingrich backs Obamacare's individual mandate requiring health insurance. Appearing on NBC's *Meet the Press*, Gingrich told host David Gregory that he continues to advocate for a plan he first called for in the early 1990s as a Congressman, which requires every uninsured citizen to purchase or acquire health insurance.

In 1995, Newt delivered a speech to the Center for Strategic and International Affairs in which he blames the US Constitution for making America's role in leading the world more difficult. "The American challenge in leading the world is compounded by our Constitution..."

Robert Francis "Beto" O'Rourke

Congressman Robert Francis "Beto" O'Rourke: Strange Stories

He calls himself "Beto" to give his presidential candidacy a Mexican-American flavor. Age 46, he sometimes rides on-stage on a skateboard, wearing jeans and an open-neck sports shirt. His family is well-to-do and like most political psychopaths, he's never had real jobs, but now wants to be President of the United States. He tried for the U.S. Senate in Texas in 2018, but lost by a squeaker to Senator Ted Cruz.

He was a member of a punk rock band for some years where he wore a woman's dress. He hacked people's computers as a member of a weird cult group, the "Cult of the Dead Cow."

O'Rourke hit another vehicle while driving drunk on his 26th birthday, but fled the scene. He's ideologically a socialist.

At age 15, Beto wrote a revealing fantasy short story in which he imagined himself deriving great pleasure from driving a car and purposefully running over and killing young children outside playing.

ROBERT 'BETO' O'ROURKE TO FARMERS: GIVE 'FAIR SHARE' OF CROPS FOR CLIMATE CHANGE

f 7,245 ✉ EMAIL 🖶 SHARE 🐦 TWEET

Source: Beto O'Rourke / Facebook

by MICHELLE MOONS | 8 Apr 2019 | Washington, DC | 9,433

Democrat 2020 presidential candidate Robert "Beto" O'Rourke proposed Friday in Iowa that the U.S. "allow" farmers to give up their "fair share" of crops to fight climate change.

O'Rourke stood aloft as he proclaimed his message at a rally in Marshalltown, Iowa Friday:

If we allow farmers to earn a profit in what they grow, if we allow them to contribute their fair share in combatting Climate Change by growi

Beto wore a dress while a member of the punk rock band, The El Paso Pussycats.

Beto is a socialist. Here is just one of his nutty ideas.

The story detailed the narrator's murder spree, as part of his goal seeking "the termination of everything that was free and loving." The piece described his first kill as the murder of two children crossing the street. It reads:

"Then one day, as I was driving home from work, I noticed two children crossing the street. They were happy, happy to be free from their troubles.

I knew, however, that this happiness and sense of freedom were much too overwhelming for them. This happiness was mine by right. I had earned it in my dreams. As I neared the young ones, I put all my weight on my right foot, keeping the accelerator pedal on the floor until I heard the crashing of the two children on the hood, and then the sharp cry of pain from one of the two. I was so fascinated for a moment, that when after I had stopped my vehicle, I just sat in a daze, sweet visions filling my head.

My dream was abruptly ended when I heard a loud banging on the front window. It was an old man, who was using his cane to awaken me. He might have been a witness to my act of love. I was not sure, nor did I care. It was simply ecstasy. As I drove home, I envisioned myself committing more of these 'acts of love,' and after a while, I had no trouble carrying them out. The more people I killed, the longer my dreams were... I had killed nearly 38 people by the time of my twenty-third birthday, and each was more fulfilling than the last."

He wrote this sick piece under the name, Psychedelic Warlord. In another piece, he took on a self-proclaimed neo-nazi who maintained that Hitler was misunderstood and didn't personally want Jews killed. O'Rourke and a Jewish friend questioned the man about his theories and let him ramble about Jews and African Americans, an attempt to let him hang himself with his own words. "We were trying to see what made him think the horrible things that he did," he wrote in the piece. It is unclear whether the piece reflected a real interview, or was fictional.

Democrat Party Operatives and Other Psychopaths

From sexual deviancy to political skullduggery, Democratic Party operatives were apart of the elite Marxist category are also, in the author's opinion, psychopaths. Perhaps these disgraceful have not directly murdered anyone, nevertheless, they fit many of the characteristics of psychopaths outlined in this book. I give only a brief outline of these political psychopaths.

Jeffrey Epstein

Jeffrey Epstein was one of the worst pedophiles in American history. He developed relationships with hundreds of politicians, actors, and actresses who participated with him in depraved activities. He owned an entire island in the Caribbean, a $56 million apartment in New York City, and a sprawling hideaway New Mexico ranch. He hired 'recruiters' to go out and bring back 12-17 year old girls and shared these girls with his celebrity friends. Epstein was a wealthy man with connections in Israel

Jeffrey Epstein shown here with four of his many young victims.

On an island in the Caribbean Jeffrey Epstein built this Temple of Evil where young girls were taken, sexually assaulted and mistreated. Epstein had incredible political connections, especially in the Democratic Party. Among the political psychopaths who flew with Epstein on his "Lolita Express" aircraft to this island in the exploitation of these victims were, reportedly, former President Bill Clinton, actor Robert DeNiro, and Prince Andrew of Great Britain.

and the United States. Epstein was arrested in 2019 and jailed by U.S. Department of Justice. While awaiting trial, he was murdered in his cell by unknown assailants.

Harvey Weinstein

Harvey Weinstein is an American film producer and co-founder of Miramax Studios, which produced many successful films. Weinstein was celebrated by the Hollywood community and by Washington Democrats. In 2018, Weinstein was arrested and awaits trial for the rape and forced seduction of an untold number of starlets. Weinstein should probably be placed in the political category because of his many Democratic political connections.

Harvey Weinstein with his good friends Hillary Clinton and Gwyneth Paltrow.

Sexual deviant Harvey Weinstein, shown here with actor and film director Woody Allen. Allen has, himself, faced accusations of sexual improprieties.

Adam Schiff

Adam Schiff (D-CA) is Chairman of the House of Representatives Intelligence Committee. His psychopathic activities include repeated lying and the production of hoaxes in vain attempts to overthrow the Republican President, Donald Trump.

Nancy Pelosi

Nancy Pelosi, Speaker of the House of Representatives, and a cohort of Congressman Schiff, is a well-known liar and political fixer. In a vain attempt to unseat President Trump, Pelosi invented the Russia Hoax then followed it up with the fake Ukrainian scandal. It turns out that Pelosi's own son is an executive of a Ukrainian gas company. She is involved with many corrupt activities and apparently has no sympathy for the homeless and poor of San Francisco, hundreds of whom live within a mile of Pelosi's gated estate.

Psychopaths Lie Because They Have No Conscience. Therefore, the Truth is Not In Them

> *"Pilate therefore said unto him, Art thou a king then? Jesus answered, Thou sayest that I am a king. To this end was I born, and for this cause came I into the world, that I should bear witness unto the truth. Everyone that is of the truth heareth my voice.*
>
> *Pilate saith unto him, what is truth?..."*

Having rejected Jesus and His Truth, many Americans today are liars. Perceiving this, and being quick to take advantage of it, our Presidents also lie to us. Constantly. And our Presidents are generously rewarded for their Big Lies.

Pilate, the Roman Governor, was an educated man. No doubt he knew of the teachings of Aristotle, Diogenes, and Plato. But of Christ he knew nothing. Christ was indeed the way, the truth, and the life, but of this, Pilate was seemingly unaware. Therefore, when Jesus told Pilate, "Every one that is of the truth heareth my voice," Pilate, puzzled, said back to him, "What is truth?"

Saying this, Pilate went forth immediately unto the waiting Jews, and declared of Jesus: *"I find no fault in him."*

Pilate, therefore, sought to release Jesus, but the Jews were adamant, demanding that Pilate crucify him.

Big Lies

We are bombarded, front, sides, and back by lies of our leaders. They are psychopaths and lying is, for them, a much cherished perpetual deed. President Obama knowingly lied to us about ObamaCare: *"If you like your doctor, you can keep your doctor. If you like your medical care plan..."*

Obama's health-care adviser, Jonathan Gruber, MIT Professor, revealed recently that Obama and his team knew that the American people are "stupid" and so, drafted the bill with a multitude of obscure language to conceal its horrific effects on our lives. As Congresswoman Nancy Pelosi admitted, "We have to pass the Bill in order to find out what is in it."

Psychopath President Bill Clinton—Bombing Tylenol Plants

As President, lies rolled off Bill Clinton's lips like molasses. Remember: "I never had sex with that woman." He was referring to Monica Lewinsky, with whom he did have sex: Oral sex, phone sex, etc.

When questioned, Clinton equivocated, playing semantics with us: "Well, it all depends on what 'is' is," he responded.

To distract people's attention from the Lewinsky mess, President Clinton ordered the U.S. Air Force to bomb and destroy a factory in the Sudan which, he claimed, was manufacturing *"weapons of mass destruction (WMDs)."*

He knew, and we the citizens, subsequently discovered, that the demolished factory was producing not WMDs, but Tylenol pills.

President Bill Clinton lied when he said, "I did not have sexual relations with that woman—Ms. Lewinsky.

More on President and Psychopath George W. Bush

George W. Bush was a consummate liar. He lied about serving in the National Guard during Vietnam. He and his diabolical Vice President, Dick Cheney, lied about WMDs in Iraq. They even enlisted the help of Great Britain to lie about "intelligence" pointing to WMDs in Iraq. This lie alone resulted in many thousands of American service men and women dying or losing limbs in a grotesque war to stop Saddam Hussein from employing those non-existent "mushroom cloud" atomic bombs against the U.S. Homeland. We went on to massacre some 500,000 Iraqis and had Saddam Hussein hung.

And our lying former Secretary of State, Madeleine Albright, asked about this carnage, stated, "It was worth it." (See Wesley Clark Article, *Power of Prophecy*, Feb. 2006).

Obama, Clinton, Bush are all psychopaths. As psychopaths, each is a charismatic, compulsive liar with absolutely no conscience, and no remorse.

President George W. Bush knowingly lied about Weapons of Mass Destruction in Iraq.

Lies Gave Us Mass Slaughter—The Stories of Presidents Wilson, Roosevelt, and Truman

Their terrible lies followed a pattern set long ago by Presidents Woodrow Wilson and Franklin Roosevelt. Wilson lied to us to get us in World War I. He claimed that the Germans had sunk an unarmed passenger liner in the Atlantic, the Lusitania, with great loss of American lives. In fact, we now know that the Lusitania carried armaments for Germany's opponent, Great Britain, and its armed forces. Further, the Lusitania was sent directly into harm's way by Wilson and his chief adviser, Rothschild puppet Colonel Mandel House. The reason: So that Americans would be angry enough to prosecute a war.

The Lusitania passenger liner was filled with armaments for Great Britain and was sent directly into harm's way by President Woodrow Wilson.

The American people also were bamboozled because of *lies* told by Wilson to the effect that an Income Tax, if approved, would never affect more than the richest two percent of Americans, and that a Federal Reserve System would be best in managing our economy.

In 1913, the Internal Revenue Service and the Federal Reserve System began, and the American citizenry has suffered great loss ever since.

President Franklin D. Roosevelt was one of the greatest liars of all time. He schemed and lied to cause a reluctant U.S. to go to war. History now reveals that Roosevelt and his advisers knew *before the event* of the Japanese attack planned at Pearl Harbor. They knew and withdrew three great aircraft carriers from Pearl Harbor so that America would still have war-making capability in the Pacific.

Poor Admiral Kimmel, leader of U.S. Forces at Pearl Harbor, took the brunt of the criticism for the supposedly "surprise" attack. He was court-martialed and dismissed from the Navy. But in the late 1990s, a half-century later, congressional committees secretly met with the Kimmel family. Seeing the grave misjustice done by FDR, the Congress privately voted to give the Admiral, now dead, a belated pardon.

Still, most Americans today continue to believe the lie of FDR that Pearl Harbor was a surprise attack. Pearl Harbor was an intentional human sacrifice, a holocaust that consumed the lives of over 2,400 innocents.

At the close of World War II, we were repeatedly lied to again. First, we were lied to when it turned out that Roosevelt had voluntarily surrendered half of Europe to madman, Soviet monster Joseph Stalin.

Then, we were lied to about the Nazis who were punished at Nuremberg for war crimes. That lie was accomplished by our hideous *torture* of the defeated Nazis. When you are beaten viciously, branded on the back by hot irons, and your fingernails pried loose by screwdrivers, you'll confess almost anything it seems.

Then, during Truman's Administration, rather than assist the broken German nation to recover, we delayed that recovery by General Eisenhower's horrible punishing of millions of innocent men, women, and children with our satanic Morgenthau Plan. Read Thomas Goodrich's book, *Hellstorm*, to learn of America and Russia's beneficent leadership. Or study the murder of General George Patton, who had refused to cooperate further with the Morgenthau postwar death plan for Germany.

Very soon, thanks to modern-day psychopaths, you and I could be sitting in jail cells, moaning about how we've been lied to. It will be too late, then. *It might already be too late.*

FBI Miscreants

From 2015-2017, attempts by Deep State operatives in the Department of Justice and

President Harry S. Truman, for almost 3 years, allowed the murderous Morgenthau Plan to punish millions of innocent men, women, and children in defeated Germany.

FBI gave us clear examples of psychopathic individuals. These left-over individuals of the Obama Administration attempted a secret coup to unseat President Donald Trump. Their treachery and willingness to indict innocent people and to rig the 2016 election by covering up crimes of Hillary Clinton are examples of their psychopathic behavior. Among these psychopathic criminals are FBI director James Comey, assistant FBI director Andrew McCabe, and high-ranking FBI agents Peter Strzok and Lisa Page. In their failed attempt to remove President Trump from office they enlisted the aid of former FBI director Robert Mueller, who spent two and one-half years and some 35 million dollars in his devious work as Special Counsel.

Assisted by 14 Democrat Department of Justice attorneys, former FBI director Robert Mueller spent two and one-half years and $35 millions investigating the false allegations that President Trump was an active agent of Russian President Vladimir Putin.

FBI Director James Comey and his Assistant Director, Andrew McCabe proved to be "bad cops" who allegedly conspired in a coup to unseat Donald Trump as President. Both were fired.

Lisa Page, FBI lawyer, fired for her criminal behavior in the plot to overthrow President Donald Trump.

Chapter Fifteen

The Revolution and Its End

"In a revolution, as in a novel, the most difficult part to invent is the end."

—Alexis de Tocqueville

Michael Krieger, writing in his internet blog (*LibertyBlitzkrieg* blog), warned of a growing struggle for global power between Red China and the United States. It is about geographical power, said Krieger, and both China and the United States are on a major collision course. But, wrote Krieger, "What's most fascinating about this period of time" is that "there is another great struggle happening, arguably much more important...which centers around a conflict between decentralization and centralization, between freedom and top-down control."

The gathering of psychopaths is at hand. The *Crazy Times* era is fast upon us, and world chaos and national survival are at stake. Psychopaths at the national and group level are demanding centralization, top-down control. Individual freedom for us all is at risk.

Psychopaths and Change

Psychopaths insist on change; they cannot tolerate free speech and individual freedoms and invent new barriers of control.

We now have a president, Donald Trump, who offers to tackle the psychopaths head-on. He is the Disrupter amidst a sea of change agents. These change agents demand that everything change, that the revolution be reconsidered and revised, that American sovereignty be ended and borders erased, and that the middle class, the normals, surrender to the superior intellect of the elite and its cultural domination.

As Krieger reports, "The 2016 election of Donald Trump was the final straw as far as the status quo's (e.g., the elite's) tolerance for free speech on the internet. It was, they surmised correctly, rumblings on the internet which had inspired the desperate Deplorables to vote for the Disrupter, Donald Trump, the man on the White Horse. The elite was only inches away from total victory. If only Hillary had won, their conquest would have been assured."

Trump's surprising and unexpected win in 2016 was a total shock to psychopaths and their legions of progressive change artists. With the internet's freedom and the

Disrupter in the White House, the psychopaths and their puppets were denied the treasure they had long strived for—the total domination of America.

A Shock to the Elite

The rising up of the beleaguered middle class, the Deplorables, and their defeat of the coastal elite (west and east coasts) by their underdog election win of Donald Trump have caused ripples of bitter anger amongst the elite. This has especially affected the media, entertainment celebrities, the university faculties, the moguls who own the social engines (Google, Twitter, Yahoo, Facebook, Amazon, etc.), and the deep state bureaucrats. These are the primary movers and shakers in the elite world, and virtually all are extremist liberals, progressives, and socialists.

The elite hate God, despise Christians, detest blue-collar and working-class Americans, and hold the United States in contempt. They greatly favor globalizing and strive for a New World Order, to be built on the aching backs of ordinary American citizens. They snicker at such notions as *America First*, promote racial and religious diversity, promote sexual promiscuity and abortion, and dishonor the flag and our nation's founding fathers.

The psychopaths are leaders in this revolt against tradition and want change because they are psychologically unfit to live and prosper in the normal world. They want to create a new world, where they dominate, where they set the rules, one where the normal people (in this case, the "Deplorables") are watched, spied on, and ruled over. In essence, a slave state of Big Brother proportions, which is fast becoming a reality with artificial intelligence, computers, biotechnology, and ubiquitous cameras.

Pat Buchanan, conservative and traditionalist, notes in a recent column, *"Is the American Century Over for Good?"*:

> "Trump is denounced for calling the media the enemy of the people. Yet that media in news columns, as well as editorials, routinely describes him as a racist, sexist, xenophobe, homophobe, Islamaphobe, and bigot... Those headlines reveal not only the news judgement of one editor, but the agenda of the elite who turn to them every morning...

> "That agenda is the breaking of the president; his disgrace and fall... Our so-called Dreamers in Washington, D.C. look to the triumphant return to power of the establishment the American people threw out in 2016."

> "The alliance that seeks to bring down Trump is formidable," says Buchanan, and includes "deep state leakers and media collaborators, the Democratic Party and House, most of America's commentariat, and the cultural elites in the arts, academia, and Hollywood."

Buchanan fails to mention the psychopathic luminaries that predominate among the elite, though I suspect he is well aware that they exist. They represent the centralized power possessed by the establishment, the elite who now rule over us. They are growing stronger each day.

Now is the Time of Monsters

Antonio Gramsci, Italian philosopher and a Marxist/Socialist, said it best when, describing the psychopath era, he stated:

"The old world is aging, and the new world struggles to be born; now is the time of monsters."

Laura Knight-Jadczyk the publisher who wrote the brilliant introduction to Lobaczewski's perceptive work, *Political Ponerology*, explains that Lobaczewski's book was published to help readers "understand what was happening in a world gone completely mad." She was speaking, of course, of the insane world of Soviet-era Communism. But she was also warning of a world gone mad under the tutelage of the United States of America. This, indeed, is the "new world struggling to be born," the world that threatens to bring forth from the feral darkness "the time of monsters."

Let each of us who cares about our fellow man and the future of family and nation pray and endeavor to prevent that struggling new world, the time of monsters, from damaging our lives and our posterity. We who are normal must all work together to stop the psychopaths and end the emergence of America as a Psychopath Nation.

Index

About the Author

Well-known author of three #1 national bestsellers, Texe Marrs has written books for such major publishers as Simon & Schuster, John Wiley, Prentice Hall/Arco, McGraw-Hill, and Dow Jones-Irwin.

Texe Marrs was assistant professor at the University of Texas at Austin for five years. He has also taught international affairs, political science, and psychology for two other universities. A graduate *summa cum laude* from Park College, Kansas City, Missouri, he earned his Master's degree at North Carolina State University.

As a career USAF officer (now retired), he commanded communications-electronics and engineering units. He holds a number of military decorations including the Vietnam Service Medal and Presidential Unit Citation, and has served in Germany, Italy, and throughout Asia.

For More Information

Our Newsletter

Power of Prophecy offers a *free* printed newsletter focusing on world events, false religion, and secret societies, cults, and the occult challenge to Christianity. If you would like to receive this newsletter, please write to:

Power of Prophecy
4819 R.O. Drive, Suite 102
Spicewood, Texas 78669

You may also e-mail your request to:
customerservice1@powerofprophecy.com

Our Websites

The *Power of Prophecy* newsletter is published free each month on the following websites. Explore the exciting website packed with interesting, insight filled articles, videos, breaking news, and other information delving into conspiracies and cover-ups, exposing the elite agenda in opposition to American freedom, and proclaiming Jesus Christ as Lord and Saviour. Descriptions of all Texe Marrs' books and the books of many other informative authors are available. You also have the opportunity to order an exciting array of books, tapes, and videos through *Power of Prophecy's* online *Catalog and Sales Stores*. Visit the websites at:

www.powerofprophecy.com
www.conspiracyworld.com

Our Internet and Shortwave Radio Program

Power of Prophecy's international radio program, *Power of Prophecy*, is broadcast weekly on shortwave radio throughout the United States and the world. *Power of Prophecy* can be heard on WWCR at 4.840 on Sunday nights at 9:00 p.m. Central Time. You may also listen to *Power of Prophecy* 24/7 on websites *powerofprophecy.com* and *conspiracyworld.com*.